POWER
OF THE
CAMPAIGN
PYRAMID

HOPE IS NOT A STRATEGY

RON WALLACE
&
WESLEY McCALL

ISBN 10: 1-59152-111-4
ISBN 13: 978-1-59152-111-2

Published by Pyramid Power Publishing, LLC
© 2013 by Ron Wallace

For more information, go to www.campaignpyramid.com or email info@campaignpyramid.com.

You may order extra copies of this book by calling Farcountry Press toll free at (800) 821-3874.

sweetgrassbooks
a division of Farcountry Press

Produced by Sweetgrass Books; PO Box 5630, Helena, MT 59604; (800) 821-3874; www.sweetgrassbooks.com.

The views expressed by the author/publisher in this book do not necessarily represent the views of, nor should be attributed to, Sweetgrass Books. Sweetgrass Books is not responsible for the content of the author/publisher's work.

Printed in the United States.

17 16 15 14 13   1 2 3 4 5

ACKNOWLEDGMENTS

"Many hands make light work." – JOHN HEYWOOD

Thank you to everyone who in some way contributed to our campaigning education through the years and made us better managers, consultants, trainers, and winners. This book would not exist without you and those experiences.

A number of people were instrumental in helping us make this book a reality and encouraged us at every step of the process. Our hats are off to you.

Our close friend, Councilman Bill Lusk, provided advice and campaign wisdom to us all along the writing journey.

Without reserve, we want to thank our editor, Janice Rutledge of Rutledge Publishing. We also appreciate the team at Sweetgrass Books, especially Will Harmon, editor, and Kathy Springmeyer, director of publications.

We owe a debt of gratitude to Ron's three co-writers on an upcoming leadership book, *Taking the Bull by the Horns;* Jim Fallon, the original energy bunny who constantly pushed us to keep going; Randy Gravitt, co-author of *Finding Your Way: Discovering the Truth About You,* and writer of the daily blog @i2ileadership.org that is read by thousands daily; and David Schiff, the founder of the Operant Group, Inc., a Human Performance Improvement consulting company and author of *The Consultant's Digest.* Bob Meyers spent endless hours making us look good. Bob is the author of a beautiful award-winning coffee table book *Bygone Treasures and Timeless Beauties: Barns of Old Milton County.* Bob and Ron are in the process of producing another coffee table book on the best Irish pubs in America.

Special thanks for contributions from Campaign Manager Fred Hicks, who owns HEG, LLC and provides an array of campaign services.

ABOUT THE AUTHORS

RON WALLACE

Ron Wallace retired from UPS as president of UPS International, where he was deeply involved with government leaders and politicians throughout the U.S. and the world. For over ten years he has served with and managed numerous political campaigns, garnering a remarkable win rate. *Power of the Campaign Pyramid* draws heavily on Ron's experience conducting campaign orientations, analyses, and trainings.

Ron's savvy and no-bones approach in both civic and business arenas have helped him serve effectively as chair of the Georgia Governor's Commission. He has also chaired or co-chaired more than thirty boards around the world prior to his retirement. Ron presently serves as a director on five boards and three charitable foundations.

WESLEY McCALL

Wesley McCall has spent several years learning the ins and outs of political campaigns and elections. He began serving as a volunteer coordinator and grew to become a sought-after campaign manager. The ability to influence people through leadership and marketing was a major focus of study for several years while earning his bachelor's degree from Grand Canyon University. Wesley's steady leadership, marketing strategy, and strong conviction to stay above the fray have helped numerous candidates win elections with clear consciences.

Wesley devotes his time to his family and volunteering as a sitting board member with several community organizations and foundations. Wesley shares his success with his lovely wife, Jakima, and their son, Ian.

TABLE OF CONTENTS

ENTERING THE PYRAMID

IT'S ALMOST THAT SEASON AGAIN. Yes, that would be *campaign* season! And this time you're ready to toss your hat into the ring. You have a gut feeling that you could win, but you're not quite sure how to get there. You begin to wonder: *How do I grow my influence and increase my impact on voters? How do I make myself the frontrunner? And why is it that some candidates seem to soar, while others barely get off the ground? What do I need to do to be the winner?*

As questions about strategy begin to swirl in your mind, you can almost hear your theme song rallying your supporters, and you can imagine the "winner" checkmark next to your name on the TV screen. Yet the big question pops into your head: *How do I get started?* That's where we can help. First, we will provide you with a Campaign Countdown Checklist to help you anticipate every step of the campaign process. Next we'll lead you through a Campaign Readiness Assessment. Then, we will introduce you to the *Power of the Campaign Pyramid,* a remarkable tool for earning the votes you need to win an election.

With a road map designed to get you to your destination, we will serve as your tour guides through the rough and tumble terrain known as modern political campaigning. Don't worry. We're not just a bunch of one-dimensional hacks armed with red ties, blue jackets, and lapel pins. You know, the kind of guys that make you duck behind a couch when you see them ringing your doorbell on a Sunday afternoon. We have extensive experience in the field, with wins in just about every type of election, and that has allowed us to develop a proven step-by-step approach to winning an election. Yes, we said "winning"—not just campaigning. The *Power of the Campaign Pyramid* is a handbook designed to stop the aimless wandering by pointing you in the right direction for political success.

Running for office is a stressful process that has been blamed for driving souls to the brink of insanity. Candidates frequently don't know where to begin on the campaign trail, how to fight through the middle of the journey, or how to finish strong. And don't bet one red cent that we are talking about novices. Most campaigners—even campaign veterans—lack one essential thing: an understanding of the principles of political campaigning. Like Newton's Laws of Thermodynamics, there are principles that give shape to the campaign universe. Abide by them and you can win. Ignore them and you will almost certainly lose.

> ### *Caution! This book is NOT hypothetical,*
> ### *nor is it based on opinion, what-ifs, or maybes.*

The *Power of the Campaign Pyramid* is based on extensive research, empirical data, and personal interviews with real winners and losers (we learned from their mistakes) to provide you with a simple step-by-step process specifying *how* you can effectively use your time, money, and talent. This one-of-a-kind book describes the campaign process from A to Z, or should we say, from Qualification to Election, putting an end to the guessing game of *how to get there.*

In addition to the campaigning secrets and wisdom we've learned and won with over the years, we also went to voters across the country with an extensive survey. Targeting likely voters, we asked them what influences their decision to vote for one candidate over another. And boy, did they give us an earful.

With an impressive win rate, we believe we have revolutionized the campaign game enough to include the most effective techniques that will allow almost anyone to win an election. You may also be surprised to learn that the most successful campaign tactics may be the least expensive.

Keep in mind that each campaign is fluid and has its own unique challenges. Whether you are a novice or a seasoned campaigner, you will discover new insights backed by real data in the pages to follow.

Embrace the lessons, don't repeat the mistakes of others, and learn how to win from the voters who will elect you.

Of course, there are no guarantees. No candidate or consultant wins them all. Sometimes you can do everything right and still lose, but very rarely can a candidate do much wrong and still win. We also know from experience that a race for elective office eventually results in a humble moment that reminds everyone that we are all human.

THE CAMPAIGN COUNTDOWN CHECKLIST

As we said, one of the first questions most candidates ask is, "How and when do I start my campaign?" But that question doesn't go far enough. An election campaign is a long, winding road with many potential potholes, roadblocks, and detours. If you look only at the first 10 feet of road, you'll be poorly prepared for the journey ahead. Far better to have a map that shows the whole route.

The *Campaign Countdown Checklist* is that map. It spells out the key steps you must take, week by week, counting backward from Election Day. The basic idea of a campaign checklist also serves as the blueprint for this book—we'll follow the checklist's general outline as we fill in the details of every step. The sample checklist we provide here is a good start, but you'll want to draft your own personal campaign countdown checklist of events, benchmarks, deadlines, meetings, and all the other numerous activities you will be engaged in. You can flesh out each week with day-by-day items on your to-do list. Your checklist will be rich with proprietary information, so share it with internal people only. It's important to stay flexible as you move through your checklist and be able to divert to higher priorities as the campaign unfolds.

It's time for the campaign countdown! Below is an example of a planning checklist. Customize yours to fit your particular plans. Start as far out as you can, and work backward from Election Day. Some candidates plan out years from Election Day, while others have to make do with a shorter time frame. Although it is possible to win an election with less time, we advocate that you start serious and detailed planning at least 20 weeks in advance.

CAMPAIGN COUNTDOWN CHECKLIST

WEEK	TASK
20	☐ Assess your campaign readiness ☐ Research your position ☐ Understand election laws ☐ Identify key dates and deadlines
19	☐ Select which office to run for ☐ Select a campaign manager ☐ Build an A-Team ☐ Begin precinct and voter history analysis ☐ Research issues in your district
18	☐ Begin training your team and volunteers ☐ Identify key financial donors ☐ Set your campaign budget ☐ Develop a marketing plan and materials ☐ Research local media contacts
17	☐ Create your platform ☐ Craft your message and talking points ☐ Order material such as signs, push cards, and door hangers
16	☐ Prepare a stump speech ☐ Develop a support team and volunteer army ☐ Plan fundraising events ☐ Compile a list of endorsements
15	☐ Announce your campaign ☐ Activate social media and website ☐ Send announcement autocalls
14	☐ Send first mailer ☐ Start a phone bank
13	☐ Increase your speaking events ☐ Establish email lists
12	☐ Start door-to-door campaign ☐ Hold meet and greets

WEEK	TASK
11	☐ Reserve media spots for the month of the election
10	☐ Make sure all financial forms are in order ☐ Make sure qualifying date is set
9	☐ Hold fundraisers
8	☐ Start placing signs throughout the district ☐ Start handing out materials at large public events ☐ Continue door-to-door
7	☐ Start weekly campaign team meetings ☐ Focus on early voters
6	☐ Release weekly key endorsements with the strongest closest to election
5	☐ Push for more sign installation ☐ Begin running print and other media ads ☐ Continue speeches at public events ☐ Assign district captains to polling locations
4	☐ Send personal letters to voters ☐ Continue sign installation to show momentum
3	☐ Start sign waving at major roads and intersections ☐ Do a big surge of sign installation ☐ Canvass school bus stops ☐ Send second mailer
2	☐ Increase sign waving ☐ Have influencers call their contacts ☐ Send get-out-the-vote messages through social media ☐ Activate phone banks and personal phone calls
1	☐ Send final mailer ☐ Strong use of social media and send email blasts day before and day of election ☐ Pickup residential signs and deliver early in the morning to the election sites ☐ Vote and host victory party!

STEP 1
ASSESS YOUR CAMPAIGN READINESS

"Man is by nature a political animal." – ARISTOTLE

ALL TYPES OF PEOPLE RUN FOR PUBLIC OFFICE, and some believe their charm alone will win them the coveted position. Sound like a good start? Not so fast. You can get by on charm for about 15 minutes. After that, you'd better know something. A few pull it off (probably with weak opposition). So, if charm is your game plan for winning an election, then go for it—overspend, overwork, and in the end pray for luck. You will need it because charm alone rarely works.

What really *works* is knowing the wants of your constituents, understanding the scope of their positions and the political landscape, knowing your own strengths and shortcomings, and being able to get the support and finances you need. *"Give them what they want so you'll be around to give them what they need."*

IS IT WORTH DOING?

A campaign is serious business: it is expensive, time consuming, and stressful. We are the first to admit these facts. There are high stakes to consider when running for public office, but there are also huge, lasting rewards. Things such as learning new skills, providing stewardship at a high level, and earning influence to create positive change in communities are all great rewards most candidates seek.

It is no small feat to engage in the brutal contest that is modern political warfare. This challenge is especially true in today's 24/7 news cycle where a highly informed electorate demands a steady stream of timely information. The public is inundated with information from social media, which provides a platform for instantaneous political discourse. The next campaign season seems to start before the current one ends.

When the polls close and the votes are counted, every campaign team sits around the war room with the same questions. The winners want to know what caused the victory and the losers want to know why they lost. Explaining a loss is usually easy, with the obvious question being, "Did we beat ourselves?"

What is it, though, that brings about a victory? What lures the voters into the winner's camp? What motivates the masses to choose one candidate over the others? Does the answer lie in planting all those campaign signs? Is it sending campaign mailers? Could it be those aggravating phone calls? What about debates or knocking on doors? Does the difference lie in volunteers holding signs on Election Day, or is it email blasts and social media? How about early and absentee voting? Did creating the database help? Did polling bring value? How about the voter lists? Did the blizzard of car magnets, decals, or colorful t-shirts do the trick? Do this, do that, and you will win. Sounds easy enough, right? Not by a long shot. The term *political science* is very misleading. Why? Because something that is scientific is absolute, or at least well established. But in this case, you are dealing with circumstances and public opinion that can change quickly, many times for no logical reason. Although the tactics are similar, every campaign is its own unique beast.

As a candidate, you will be challenged to bring an intelligent and inspiring message to explain why you will be more effective than your opponents. Every word you speak will be subject to scrutiny. Do you know the issues? Can you communicate them effectively? Can you counter your opponents' arguments while developing your own? It will be tough.

Meanwhile, your entire life becomes an open book for the public to judge. You will become a focal point for the media and your opponents—your family (or absence of one), religion, politics, and ancestry will all come into question. Add to that your finances, homes, cars, pets, and hobbies, your attire, and your personality—all will be put on stage for the entire world to see. Is running for office worth all of the effort, sacrifices, and intrusions? Is the win going to be positive for your family, your community, and you? These are questions that only you can answer.

However, before you shout a resounding "Yes!" consider this. Our experience tells us the first thing a candidate should do before entering a race is to assess his or her campaign readiness by answering a number of important questions. The following will serve as your *Campaign Readiness Assessment*. Spend some time giving careful consideration to each question before you move forward with your quest.

1. *Why am I running?*
2. *Do I have the time?*
3. *Do I have the money?*
4. *Is my house in order?*
5. *Do I have enough help?*
6. *Is my family supportive?*
7. *Do I have skeletons in my closet?*
8. *Am I healthy enough?*
9. *Am I qualified?*
10. *Do I have the support of community "influencers"?*

Why *Am I* Running?

Have you lost your mind? Are you suffering a midlife crisis? Have delusions of grandeur set in? After all, you are about to embark on a journey where the hours are long, the pay is bad, and the critics are out for blood.

> The person with big dreams is more powerful than the one with all the facts.

Before you do anything else, take some time to ask yourself, "Why *am I* running?" The question must be answered from your personal perspective. Consider the following:

- If your answer does not begin and end with what you are going to do for your community, please reconsider.

- If you are running because you want to "be" someone or because friends are whispering in your ear that they think you are the best person for the job, think again: these are not valid reasons to run for office.
- If you are running solely because you are upset with one issue, decision, or vote by an existing elected official, take a deep breath, forget your imaginary political career, and save yourself a ton of money.
- It may sound hokey, but holding public office should be about public service.

We consider the question of *Why am I running* to be the most important for you to ask yourself, because when—*not if*—the campaign gets tough, and when the road to public office curves in unanticipated ways, you will need the inspiration and conviction of your answer. Everyone will ask you this question, so you better have a good answer. You must have fire in your belly and an unstoppable passion to win. Success is more often the result of hard work and dedication rather than talent. The person with big dreams is more powerful than the one with all the facts. If you really care, it will show. You must first believe you are the only person on earth that can make life better once you take office. After having made that decision, go after it like a hungry tiger.

A Homework Exercise
As a candidate, you will not win the election without a very concise and distilled reason for running for elected office, which is another reason why we implore you to do the following small exercise.

In no more than two sentences summarize your personal reasons for running for office. Now, write two to three sentences that clearly capture the value you will bring to the voters. Memorize your summary. Repeat it. Believe in it. Convey it to the potential voter. You will be asked this question repeatedly.

Do I Have the Time?

Campaigning for office must be treated almost like a full-time job. Other commitments, such as your family and career, will compete for your time and attention. That can be a challenge. A campaign is a marathon, not a sprint. You will get up early and stay up late. Sleep will be scarce for the duration of the campaign. The campaign will virtually own you.

Thoroughly discuss the time investment with your spouse and family. They are the ones impacted the most by a campaign. Your spouse must be as "on board" as you are, or you are about to embark on the most miserable time of your life. If your spouse is not very enthusiastic about your campaign, you'd better change his or her mind. If you can't sell your own spouse on this idea, you are never going to convince thousands of voters who don't even know you!

Based on experience, we estimate a candidate must allocate between 20 to 30 hours per week in the initial months of the campaign and 40 to 60 hours per week as the election approaches. You will need to stay close to the action, so plan for very few days off. Are you up to the challenge? Ask yourself this question more than a few times before deciding to run.

Do I Have the Money?

Raising funds is difficult and the task is even that much harder in weak economic times. Are you able to contribute your own money to sustain a formidable campaign? Now is the time to evaluate your financial health. Consult with an experienced campaign manager or other elected officials about their experiences and ask their advice regarding budgets. They will quickly tell you where they maximized returns and where they felt they wasted money. There is no need to repeat the mistakes of others.

Also, now is a good time to identify your real financial supporters—before you throw your hat in the ring. Make some initial inquiries of friends, family, and colleagues about funding support. If a lack of funding becomes painfully obvious, do not be discouraged. Instead, take time to map out a financial plan that will position you for a future race.

First-time candidates have an exceptionally difficult time raising money. That difficulty can be compounded if you're running against an incumbent. Whatever the campaign budget is, first-time candidates should be prepared to fund at least 75 percent of a local campaign. Raising more than 25 percent from others is a bonus.

Is My House in Order?

A candidate's life becomes very exposed to the public over the course of a campaign. The exposure sometimes tends to drift away from political platforms and gravitate toward a candidate's personal life. Are your finances in order? Does your home or property meet city code? Are tax filings and payments current? Do you have outstanding parking tickets or moving violations? Are you in danger of foreclosure? The list could go on, but the idea should be planted in your mind—get your house in order.

If negative information becomes public, the question will eventually surface: "How can this candidate manage large public issues when he or she can't manage his or her own personal life?" Candidates and incumbents alike have suffered public embarrassment because the media or their opponents zeroed in on financial weaknesses or failures. Weigh any issues you may have and consider whether or not they will impact your race.

Again, don't be discouraged if now is not the right time to run for office. Realize you are facing real issues that other citizens have also faced. Create a plan that will allow you to get your house in order so the next race can be yours to bring home.

Do I Have Enough Help?

Campaigns are often called races because they are a contest of speed and rivalry. Who can win the most votes in the time allotted? The truth is you cannot win this contest alone. Do you need an army? Yes! You need many people working with and for you, especially in the final weeks. Surround yourself with talented people you can trust. The inner-circle campaign team, which we fondly refer to as the "A-Team," should consist of about eight loyal people who are willing to do more than stand on the sidelines and cheer. Your A-Team must be fully committed to the mission.

Your life as a candidate will be dedicated to meeting with the voters. It is not your job to be a sign planter, designer, bookkeeper, fundraiser, or any of the other numerous tasks required in a campaign. This is where your A-Team comes in with their variety of skills. At a minimum you will need the following positions covered:

- Campaign Manager
- Treasurer
- Fundraising Manager
- Marketing Manger
- Social Media Manager
- District Captain
- Attorney
- Sign Manager

DO NOT ASSUME your friends will support you and play an active role in your campaign. You are going to have to ask them, face-to-face, if they are willing to commit to your campaign and your candidacy. You will likely be surprised to find that many of the people you thought would help will not. We'll come back to the A-Team in *Step 3: Build a Winning Team* and explain the role of each position.

Is My Family Supportive?

A gentleman, who later became one of our clients, was approached by some local citizens at a political function. During the discussion, it became clear he had thought about running for office and that some of the citizens would support him. Although he realized he had a good start on identifying his support team, he was wise to let them know he needed to talk with his family first. Later that evening he approached his wife.

"Honey," he said quietly. "It appears there are some people who would be willing to support me for the upcoming city council elections. What do you think I should . . . ."

"Do it!" she interrupted. "You'd be great at it! I can so see that! Do it!"

Obviously, he had her support. However, he wanted to make sure she was aware that the spouse campaigns just as much as the candidate. Fortunately, he was able to include his family from the start.

When our candidate discussed running for office with his employer he did not receive the same enthusiastic support. This posed a dilemma for him, and rightfully so. To resolve the conflict, he arranged a meeting with his boss and the campaign consultant who would supervise the campaign team. It was a good move, as the boss saw a potential benefit in having his employee serve in a public office, realizing it could lead to networking opportunities and other dividends.

You can have all the money in the world, bucket loads of passion, off-the-charts name recognition, a squeaky clean past, and an army of volunteers. However, if you do not have the support of your family and your employer you will have a heavy anchor around your neck. If your family or employer is on the fence, have an influential person from your team or an experienced public office holder talk to them about the process and explain to them what to expect during the campaign and the obligations of the office. Answer their questions and take the mystery away. Often, when the myths of running for office are removed, your family and employer will become your strongest allies.

Do I Have Skeletons in My Closet?

Most campaigns are based on issues. However, occasionally a negative comment about you will surface that starts the gossip, the emails, and may even draw attention from the media. It will make your blood boil, but you and your family need to be prepared to deal with it in a calm, professional manner. Understand it is just part of the ugly side of politics.

Especially resist ANY urge to respond to any blogs or negative feedback online. Do NOT get caught in this pointless banter. It will add no value to your campaign. Most of these postings will be anonymous, likely by supporters of your opposition, attempting to bait you into an embarrassing public argument or statement. Based on our research, nearly 80 percent of the people surveyed said they preferred the candidates who ran a clean campaign. *Personal* attacks against a candidate or their families turned voters off more than anything else. No matter what happens, do not give in to temptation to strike back. Don't make off-the-cuff remarks you may later regret. Make it clear to your team that you intend to run a clean campaign, and then let your consultants constructively deal with any negative attacks.

If there are any skeletons in your closet, it is best to let your family, and the campaign team, know before outsiders become aware of it. The news should not come from a nosey neighbor, or worse, the media. Your campaign staff can do early damage control, make it old news, and get on with the campaign.

Am I Healthy Enough?

Campaign schedules are grueling, and the process can be a strain on a person's mental and physical health. Lack of rest, irregular meals, extended hours, and a rigorous regimen of walking door to door can be taxing on a body. Assess your health and fitness before you enter the race. Once the campaign starts, take short "mental health" breaks to relieve stress.

Am I Qualified?

Do a personal inventory of your qualifications. What is your level of education, background, and relevant business or civic experience? Take time now to update your résumé. Include accomplishments, not just education and work experience. Include only RELEVANT items. Loading up your résumé with irrelevant stuff is distracting and will be interpreted negatively by some. Examples include hunting ("killing Bambi's mother"), skydiving and riding motorcycles ("risky behavior"), taking long walks on the beach ("dewy-eyed romantic"), flower arranging ("wimpy"). Instead, focus on how your skills and qualifications compare or contrast with the other candidates.

Do I Have the Support of Community "Influencers"?

Well in advance of your campaign, consider people you know with strong influence in the community who can help your campaign succeed. This includes people who are well-known, well-respected, and, ideally, active community members who have helped other officials get elected. Are you able to gain the support of these "influencers"? If so, you've just increased your chances of a victory. If not, begin making connections NOW!

At this point, you've weighed all of the potential gains against all potential challenges and sacrifices and have made a decision whether to move forward with your candidacy or stay out of the race. If you have decided against running for office at this time, it's time to celebrate. Celebrate the fact that you have a smorgasbord of opportunities to serve your community in other ways that may be a better fit for your family and lifestyle. Also celebrate the fact that you'll save yourself some agony and a ton of money. If, on the other hand, you have decided it is worth the risk and reward to add your name to the ballot, and you are able to answer all 10 questions in the Campaign Readiness Assessment in the affirmative, congratulations! It is time to throw your hat in the ring and go to work!

 The decision to run for office is life changing. It rates right up there with other life-changing decisions, like marriage and careers. The decision should not be taken lightly. Everyone in your life will be impacted by your decision—your spouse, your family, your fellow workers, and your friends. All are subject to the scrutiny and ramifications of your decision. It is vital at this early stage to take stock as best you can, share your plans with those around you, and carefully reach a decision.

RESEARCH YOUR POSITION

"I don't know where I'm going, but I'm on my way." – RONALD REAGAN

OKAY, YOU'VE DECIDED THAT RUNNING for public office is worth it and that you are going to be awesome at it. Hurray! So, the bubbly has been popped in celebration of the decision and your friends and family are excited about the notion of it all. Now what? It's time, if you haven't already, to learn everything you can about how government works, the role and responsibilities of the office you are seeking, and relevant election laws.

GOVERNMENT 101

If you do not have basic knowledge of government affairs, you are at a distinct disadvantage. Especially if your opponent is an incumbent, remember that they have first-hand knowledge of what happens day-to-day in their current role. The good news is it is never too late to learn some of the basics of the inner workings of your local government. Whether you're running for city, county, or state office, you should meet with government officials at the respective level. The following example looks at a local city campaign, but the same research is necessary at the county and state levels as well.

Get Face-to-Face with City Officials

It will be worth your time to scan the city website and read about the roles of the mayor, city council members, and the various departments.

Schedule a meeting with the city manager and show up with specific questions rather than a simple, "What's going on?" This will make it easier for the city manager to answer your questions. Politics has no place in a well-functioning government staff. A small dose of humility and the reassurance that you only want to learn (and have no interest in introducing politics into their work environment) will probably get you much further than a demand to know, "because you are a citizen."

There is nothing like first-hand knowledge. Ask to go on a "ride along" with a police officer and get permission to spend the day at a fire station. Try to spend time in public works, engineering, and the parks and recreation department. Meet with those responsible for finance to learn about the budget and how taxes are set. Find out how permits are processed. Talk with the code enforcement officers and the city clerk. Meet with human resources and the communications people. Attend local court proceedings. Experience it all. People in most departments are eager to tell citizens what they do.

Build Your Civic Involvement Résumé

Show up and be active in civic events, city council meetings, and workshops. Attend as many different committee meetings as you can and try to become a member of one. Committees for consideration are: the Planning Commission, Design Review Board, Board of Zoning Appeals, and the Parks and Recreation Board, to name just a few. There is no substitute for on-the-job experience. Experience gives you credibility to run for a key government office.

Meet with some of the more influential and vocal groups—school boards, business associations, military veterans, homeowners associations, churches, local sports clubs, and civic groups that are active in the community. You will quickly understand their concerns and the level of influence they wield. These groups can sway an election.

Research Local and State Election Laws

As the next great politician, it is important that you know the applicable local, county, and state election laws. This will help you avoid campaign embarrassment, disqualification, or even worse, committing a criminal act, no matter how small the infraction. Understanding these laws will not only help you navigate your campaign competently and legally, it will also give you ammunition should your opponents fall short in this area. Many a candidate has been disqualified over basic rules-related mistakes or violations. The local elections board has no patience for violators. Yet in every election, it seems several candidates get into trouble. They either don't know the rules or simply choose to ignore them. Neither is good for the health of an election bid. An election may be won, but if violations are discovered later, the victory may be short lived. If there is any area of a campaign to monitor, this is it.

Identify Key Financial Disclosure Requirements and Dates

Managing campaign finances is no small task, and this aspect of campaigns is highly regulated. Since we don't plan on visiting anyone in the poorhouse, or in jail, we advise all candidates to have a trusted, competent finance person. This isn't just our recommendation— many locales require a designated treasurer to be responsible for a campaign's financial compliance. In the meantime, and well in advance of putting your name on a ballot, know the dates and requirements for filing financial disclosures with the proper elections office in your area. The requirements may be different from state to state, county to county, or from city to city. They may even change from one election year to the next; therefore, you must investigate financial filing requirements for yourself.

6 Key Pieces of Information to Know
1. What reports must be filed.
2. What signatures are required for filing.
3. Where to file reports.
4. When to file reports.
5. What format for filing reports (paper or electronic).
6. What the consequences are for a missed deadline.

If the requirements and forms for filing financial reports cannot be found on the city, county, or state's website, call the appropriate elections office (city or county board of elections or the secretary of state) to obtain them. Representatives from one or more of these government offices should be able to answer any questions you have about filing. A competent campaign manager will be well versed on all of this and will ensure you are following the rules. It is part of his or her checklist. Set up a calendar with all the required dates and have a clear plan with benchmarks to meet deadlines.

Positioning is a Strategic Plan

On the surface, choosing the office you want to run for might seem like a no-brainer. The candidate might think, *"I believe I will make a great mayor and everyone I've talked to agrees. I'll run for mayor and be awesome."* But such superficial thinking is often the plight of the uninformed or ill-advised novice. Choosing which office to run for is part of the strategy, both short and long term. It is a short-term strategy because even a win for a lower-profile office is better than a loss for a bigger one. Also, in the short term it is important to be able to grow and build the political traction required to make notable change. It is a long-term strategy because a novice candidate needs to win a seat to gain experience for those future goals. This may be a good time to consider seeking the advice of an experienced campaign manager or political mentor.

There are more questions you must consider before you rush to add your name to an election ballot. *Can I, realistically, see myself in this position, now or in the future? Where can I be the most effective and build the most support? What position should I begin with to get to where I want to go?* Most importantly, *Can I win?* Holding office will be more than a notion and a presidential wave of the hand.

A notable example of this is U.S. Secretary of State Hillary Clinton. Whether or not we agree with her politics, we can commend her process for making her way back to White House politics. As the politically involved wife of the 42nd president of the United States, Mrs. Clinton created a buzz about her interest in the Oval Office. The truth of the matter is, before President Clinton's term ended,

Mrs. Clinton had significant exposure to the presidency and was probably more qualified than some, though technically she was not considered a politician. Without title or quantifiable experience as a politician, she was theoretically not yet qualified for the role of president. Though it may have been her aspiration to become the first woman president, she did not immediately pursue presidential candidacy. Instead, in 2000 she moved to the state of New York and was elected U.S Senator, becoming the state's first female to hold the post. She then could be considered a bona fide politician, a qualification that earned her strong support for her presidential bid in 2008.

IDENTIFY OFFICE RESPONSIBILITIES

Do you really know what your desired position entails? If not, research it to learn what the daily responsibilities are. What are the legal and financial responsibilities of the position? How far will your authority extend and where will it end? Who will be your boss and to whom will you be accountable? What departments or lateral offices would you normally network with to accomplish your duties or satisfy the issues of your constituents? Is it largely a desk job, or are you required to be out in the community? Is it a Monday through Friday 9-to-5 position, or are you expected to be available 24/7, 365 days a year? Simply put: know the job you are seeking.

RESEARCH THE POST'S PAST ACCOMPLISHMENTS

As the new kid on the block you will want to step into the political arena as a strong public servant. If you're not the new kid on the block, you'll want to continue to ably fulfill the duties of the office and think about leaving a legacy of effective service. Learning from the accomplishments of your predecessors can catapult your campaign far beyond that of your unstudied opponent and provide you with a richer, more thoughtful platform.

ANTICIPATE AND PREPARE

It's the early bird that gets the worm and without a doubt, the candidate who does the early research for the position *(that should be you)* will gain a considerable advantage in the campaign. To prepare for

Nothing of value comes without effort.

your "dream job," apply these five rules: choose wisely which office to seek; understand the responsibilities and limits of the office; know the office's greatest accomplishments; understand the hierarchy of the government you will join and how it functions; and understand the applicable election laws.

After you have accomplished the important step of solidifying your decision to become a contender for the seat, it's time to get everything set for the election win of a lifetime.

STEP 3
BUILD A WINNING TEAM

"None of us is as smart as all of us." – KEN BLANCHARD

YOU CAN'T DO IT ALL. You might be led to believe you can wear every hat and that you alone hold all of the campaign expertise. You might even swear this is true, right up to the moment your campaign begins to fall apart at the seams.

⭐ **Type-A and self-sufficient personalities seem to fall the hardest.**

When the heat is on, you will be tempted to take on more responsibility. You might find yourself spending a good portion of your time backtracking, correcting mistakes, and doing everything under the sun except the single job you should be doing: getting votes. You may think that you can do it all, but campaigning requires a team, if not an army. You might only have a small team of four or five people (believe it or not, that is the norm in local campaigns). In a perfect world, the A-Team would look like what we will describe in this chapter. However, it is not always possible to recruit volunteer managers for every function on the list. Your A-Team members may have to share duties, and you may even need to hire outside people to do some of the work. Often, out of necessity, the A-Team is made up of the candidate, his or her spouse, his or her children, and a few friends. Work with what you have.

Now, you're probably asking, "When do I start my campaign?" Establishing your campaign team and preparing your strategy should be completed well ahead of the active public campaign. Early planning, including ordering campaign materials, preparing a platform, doing research, and developing message points and checklists, etc. should be done months, if not years, in advance of a campaign. Wiser candidates plan for years, and that is a big advantage. We have seen other candidates who entered a race on a late impulse and did quite well. For some, two to three months before the kick-off meeting is enough time to select a team and begin laying the groundwork for the race. Last minute planning makes things harder, but winning is still possible. The key is to take care of the basics and get all those little time-consuming details out of the way up front. This will enable you to be well prepared to follow a plan and work on the big things.

SUPER HERO STRATEGY: *JUST ANY TEAM WON'T DO*

Build a team that is so awesome and talented that they could win an election even if you weren't around. Like mutant super heroes, they have laser-like focus. In a stormy situation, they can change the winds of the campaign in your favor. Faster than a speeding bullet, a good team can out-strategize and outwit your opponent. Like caped crusaders, they want to win the election even more than you do.

You don't need cheerleaders that can "kinda" work now and then when they have time. Put those people on the volunteer list and call them later. In this super competitive environment, your team needs to be the super heroes of political campaigning.

And as great as this all sounds, you and your campaign manager are responsible for creating that X factor. That means selecting, training, and nurturing your staff and volunteers so they can perform well beyond normal expectations. These people are your hands, feet, eyes, ears, mouth, and brains hitting the ground running with the message of your campaign.

A winning team will win elections by pushing even a lackluster or ill-prepared candidate into stardom. We're not saying that you are lackluster, but it is important to emphasize that a dedicated, high-energy team can boost the power of your campaign tremendously. On the other hand, a mediocre, uncommitted, or untrained team can greatly diminish a positive presence.

People you know, as well as complete strangers, will come forward willing to help. The challenge is to find the right skill sets. There is plenty of work to be done, and everyone should be assigned to jobs where he or she can add value. Keep in mind, most team members will have several responsibilities, and everyone will be involved in various group tasks, such as installing signs, working phone banks, walking neighborhoods, holding signs on Election Day, and the list goes on and on. Don't overwork team members or give them too many assignments, as that may take the focus off their primary responsibilities. Keep the priorities straight. Remember, they are volunteers.

TWO TIERS TO EVERY TEAM

There are two tiers to a campaign team. We will start with the inner circle, or the "A-Team," as we fondly call them. The A-Team normally consists of the candidate, campaign manager, treasurer, fundraising manager, marketing manager, social media manager, district captain, attorney, and a sign manager. It is a good idea to have a back-up person to work closely with the lead person in each job; one who can share the workload and is capable of taking over at any given moment.

The second tier, or support team, includes the all-important field of volunteers. These are the people who come in masses to install signs, help at events, hand out materials, work the phone banks, assist you as you walk the neighborhoods knocking on doors, and the many other tasks that are so critical to the campaign. Neighborhood leaders are also included in this group. Volunteers should be assigned to each team manager based on their skill level and the amount of time they are willing to spend.

LESSONS LEARNED

Before you assemble your A-Team, we feel obligated to warn you that it is not a good idea to have family members on it (although this is not always practical or preventable). Family members can, and should, play an important role in the campaign. However, if they are part of the A-Team, their presence may cause conflicts and even take away the necessary juice the A-Team needs to operate effectively. Ideally, you will find other supporters to fill the A-Team roles. There will be some strong opposing views about this recommendation, so take it for what it's worth. We won't say we told you so.

We had a wanna-be candidate who asked us to put on a training session for her newly formed campaign team. When we arrived, we went through the normal introductory session and met Mom, the campaign manager; Dad, the campaign coordinator; Brother Frank, the fundraiser; Sister Sue, the communication officer; Aunt Freda, the financial officer; and, of course, the husband, who stated that his job was to approve all decisions. Halfway through the training, egos took over and it turned into an episode of *The Family Feud*. It's yet another story of a short-lived candidate who did not get to first base. Then again, this book had not been published. So how were they to know?

THE A-TEAM

Let's look more closely at the key positions for a strong A-Team. We are not advocating that you highjack your budget for the most highly paid inner circle, hoping this will bring you winning results. With the exception of the campaign manager, the A-Team is normally made up of volunteers. We recommend finding people who 1) are competent in their specific areas of commitment, 2) will work well with other team members, 3) will enthusiastically support your mission, and, most importantly, 4) can dedicate their time.

Campaign Manager

Campaign managers are like the head coaches of sports teams. They oversee all aspects of the campaign. They work with the quarterback (candidate) and the assistant coaches (the rest of the A-Team) to set the campaign strategy. The assistant coaches are the brains and muscle behind the scenes. Therefore, the head coach must rely heavily on them to execute their planned strategies. Although the campaign manager will oversee all team members, the majority of this manager's time needs to be spent with the candidate.

Depending on the strength of the assistant coaches, the campaign manager will normally guide and approve all critical elements throughout the campaign. These elements include managing voter contacts, public appearances, press releases, debate preparation, all written campaign material, fundraising, platforms, and message points. He or she will perform the precinct and voter analyses, oversee budgets, manage all phases of marketing, and, of course, train the A-Team and work closely with them throughout the campaign. In this critical role, the campaign manager should have the ability to perform all functions of a campaign. The campaign manager will ensure the campaign is firing on all cylinders and that timelines are being met.

If you are looking for a campaign manager, go shopping. Get input from local office holders and let them tell you who they would or wouldn't use. If possible, use a local campaign manager because he or she will have a feel for the community and will be more accessible. The best ones, with consistent win records, will command a higher fee. But remember, using a campaign manager is an investment, not a cost. They will save you money because of their network and will practically pay for themselves. Above all, make sure this person has the time and is committed to YOUR campaign (and not another client's) for the long run.

If you cannot afford a paid campaign manager, then seek out someone who is politically savvy, perhaps a former office holder who has run campaigns in the past.

Treasurer

The treasurer receives deposits and discloses contributions, makes and discloses expenditures, and files periodic reports of campaign finance activity. He or she must establish clear policies for all payments and monetary transactions and ensure the campaign's compliance. Check your state's requirements. Normally, any reasonable accounting procedure may be employed by the treasurer or finance manager to ensure a full, complete, and accurate account of all financial and disclosure information. The treasurer must preserve all records and accounts for a stipulated amount of time after each periodic report has been filed.

Early in the campaign, the campaign manager, candidate, treasurer, and other key members of the team should develop business and financial plans. The treasurer ensures that the plans are followed earnestly and that funds are available to support the campaign. The treasurer will be responsible for filing appropriate disclosure reports with the city, county, or state *before* the scheduled deadlines.

Fundraising Manager

Fundraising is a true art. It is not easy to ask for money, especially for political reasons, but it has to be done. That is why the fundraising manager is so valuable to a campaign. A fundraising manager is responsible for researching and soliciting funding from individuals and businesses whose interests align with the campaign and for coordinating all fundraising logistics, including the use of volunteers. For this reason, there is a big advantage if some of your fundraisers are well known in the community. The experienced fundraisers on the team generally prove to be motivators and teachers to the other volunteers. As a result, other team members and volunteers learn how to raise funds by leveraging their relationships with organizations, friends, and neighbors. Raising money, and lots of it, is the only role of this A-Team member; do not expect him or her to perform other campaign duties. By the way, EVERY person on the team should contribute to the task of raising funds for the campaign, including making their own financial contributions. Remember, volunteers who also contribute money have real skin in the game and are more motivated to see their investment succeed.

Money drives a campaign's communications by getting the candidate's message to the voters. To secure those finances, it is always best to receive donor contributions instead of financing your own campaign. It shows support from the public and avoids the image of buying votes just because you can. Also, how a campaign is funded is public knowledge. The media seeks stories about campaign funding and how the money is spent. How wisely a candidate spends money during the campaign speaks to his or her likely fiscal sense once in office.

Marketing Manager (aka Communications Manager)

The marketing manager sets marketing strategies to meet campaign objectives. He or she will play a vital role in developing the candidate's platform and message. The marketing manager must know community issues before executing the marketing strategies.

The primary objective is to sell the candidate to the voters by the most effective means. This might include traditional channels like radio, TV, and newspaper ads. It may also include sending out videos, pictures, emails, and press releases. The marketing manager will develop push cards, door hangers, and campaign mailers. Political campaigns operate in a new, noisy, world. Social media is the latest, greatest marketing tool on the planet—"use it or lose it" (the election, that is). Marketing managers, using all these tools, work closely with the candidate, campaign manager, attorney, and the social media guru to sell the candidate to the voters. If you think about it, campaigning is really nothing more than marketing. You have to sell buyers on a product or service, in this case you sell voters on the candidate.

Social Media Manager

The social media manager creates and updates campaign websites and communicates using Twitter, Facebook, blogs, phone apps, and pertinent links to and from other digital media. Today, people want instant, updated information at the touch of a button, and social media connects you to them. It has brought marketing and campaigning to a whole new level. It is inexpensive, and it gets you noticed. In campaigns, social media will set the stage for the candidate to get noticed beyond your wildest imagination. Digital communication must present the candidate's message in a way that is consistent with his or her printed communications. The social media and marketing managers must work closely together to deliver the consistent and fresh communications that voters expect.

District Captain

The district captain is responsible for recruiting neighborhood leaders who will build relationships within their respective neighborhoods. Priority should be given to the top voting districts and neighborhoods. The district captain and neighborhood leaders should concentrate on turning out voters in neighborhoods where you have strong support as well as among undecided voters. Done right, this will pull swing voters to your side, as well as get some voters to switch camps. Those who don't know the candidates need a push, best delivered by so-called grassroots campaigns. Hearing from their neighbors and other influencers will bring many uncommitted voters to your side of the fence—it all goes back to the human contact tactic. There are many ways to do this, but regardless of how it is done, the strategy of one-on-one contact rests at the heart of the Pyramid Principle.

Attorney

The attorney should approve all information going out to the public and should be readily available to advise your campaign team on important matters. Ideally, the position would be filled by a volunteer, like any other A-Team member, but the person must be an actual attorney. He or she will help write, or at least approve, all documents and financial records to ensure they are in compliance with local laws and regulations. Your attorney will also handle any legal challenges filed against you, or any you choose to file. It would be best to find an attorney who has an understanding of the political arena.

Sign Manager

The sign manager, preferably a workaholic with never-ending energy, is responsible for tracking yard sign requests and ensuring that signs are installed in a timely manner. He or she also coordinates sign waving at local events and posting signs at locations where the candidate will appear. One of this manager's most important missions is to ensure that signs are placed at polling locations on Election Day and that the plan for sign waivers is followed. Your sign manager must understand the local ordinances and know where signs are allowed and where they are restricted. The sign manager and his or her large volunteer team are responsible for placing as many signs as possible in key locations. A big part of their job is to find those key locations, get permission from the landowners, and plant the sign. Much of their best work may happen late at night and into the early morning hours.

> Build a team that is so awesome and talented that they could win an election even if you weren't around.

SUPPORT TEAM FUNCTIONS

Neighborhood Leaders

Each neighborhood leader is responsible for delivering the vote by working closely with the district captain. Neighborhood leaders should be well known and respected among their neighbors. The strategies vary by neighborhood, but may include setting up block parties to meet the candidate, writing letters and emails, arranging the candidate's participation in homeowner association meetings, identifying signage opportunities, and planning special events. They can also be key players at school bus stops, where they have a captive audience of parents (more on this tactic later). A strong, active neighborhood leader has the opportunity to bring more votes than you can imagine. Don't underestimate the importance of this critical position. Many of your volunteers can also be assigned as neighborhood leaders as they are likely well known in their neighborhoods. This gives them a specific job while waiting to be called on to perform other duties.

Volunteers-at-Large

Volunteers-at-large assist team leaders with whatever tasks need to be carried out: mailings and other administrative tasks, canvassing, sign waving, phone banks, polling, placing signs, working at events, etc. Some volunteers will work throughout the campaign, while others may serve only occasionally. Carefully screen volunteers. This is the easiest position for the opposition to insert spies as undercover operatives. Too dramatic? It happens more often than you might think.

BUILD VOLUNTEER LISTS

As you talk to friends, family, co-workers, neighbors, and other supporters, ask for their help as a volunteer, and then ask them to bring others to the volunteer team. It is okay to be greedy. The larger the volunteer army, the better. Create a database of potential volunteers. Remember, everyone who says he or she wants to help may not be available when needed. Until a person is confirmed for a task, he or she is only a potential volunteer. It's just amazing how many people get amnesia when it comes time to do real work. Be sure to include in the database names, phone numbers, addresses, skills and abilities, areas of interest for volunteering, financial and material contributions, and referrals to other potential volunteers. Also list any prior campaign experience and roles served. Assign one person the role of overseeing the volunteers and regularly updating them on the campaign's progress. Let them know key dates and invite them to help whenever they can. Simply attending campaign functions will keep their enthusiasm high. Do not take them for granted. There is always plenty of work, and it's important to keep them engaged. All of them will be vote getters, fundraisers, and on-the-ground workers IF they know they are an important part of your campaign team. They are all MVPs and the backbone of every successful campaign. Your A-Team can only do so much and will appreciate all the help they can get.

TRAINING

Training is one of the most important factors for building a winning team. Your team has one shot to propel you into election history. Training shows them how.

All team members should be clear on the campaign platform,

your values, their respective roles, and the campaign strategy, goals, and timelines. The campaign manager and candidate will work with each team leader to determine specific goals.

Have your entire team, including your volunteers, read this book. It provides a proven process that will quickly get teams up to speed and help them understand the basics of running a campaign the right way.

To get the team off to a good start, the campaign manager should take the candidate and the A-Team through some basic

★ INITIAL MUST-DO TRAINING

1. Campaign strategy
2. Campaign goals
3. Goals of respective functions
4. Team manager responsibilities
5. Timelines
6. What NOT to do
7. How each team member relates to other members
8. Elections laws and campaign protocol
9. Best ways to communicate with internal team members, external groups, and the public
10. How to measure success
11. Who is in charge
12. Understanding precinct analysis
13. Understanding the voter history list
14. How to deal with disagreements

training during the first few meetings. The campaign manager should ensure that the team understands campaign laws and regulations. He or she should go into great depth on the basics of "what to do" and, *more importantly*, "what not to do" during the campaign. Introducing the precinct analysis along with the most recent voter history will also be an important part of the training. We will discuss that later.

COMMITTEE TRAINING

Each manager will be responsible for training his or her volunteer teams. For example, the sign manager will train the sign committee on the proper way to install signs. He or she will make sure they understand the many campaign sign regulations.

Campaign Kickoff Meeting
The non-public campaign starts with the first A-Team meeting and moves

ahead quickly from there. The campaign kickoff meeting is not the time to discover that you have players who don't have a feel for participating in a campaign. We find that even seasoned campaign volunteers are fairly clueless about what really works, which is why you must build and train your team far in advance of the live, public campaign.

Staying on Plan with Team Meetings

Team meetings ensure that the campaign is moving forward based on the progress of each function. Meetings also allow team members to collaborate, raise questions that are beneficial to everyone, make group decisions, encourage one another, and share information and successes. Ensure meetings are productive and well attended by adhering to the following guidelines.

10 Rules to Stay on Plan with Team Meetings

1. Start and end on time. You MUST respect your team's time.
2. Keep communications within the team honest, open, and frequent.
3. Organize meetings with an agenda.
4. Hold meetings only as needed.
5. Schedule meetings well in advance and be consistent so members can plan. For example, meet at 7 p.m. every Tuesday at the same location.
6. Each team member must come to meetings prepared to share his or her progress.
7. Respect your team by having short, productive meetings. Cut out the war stories and get to the point.
8. Hold your discussions close to the vest. Be careful with whom you share information. *Loose lips sink ships* and can bury a campaign in a hurry.
9. As an A-Team member, the campaign attorney should attend so he or she can keep abreast of what the team is doing.
10. Each member should report on the status of his or her checklist, results, and upcoming plans.

Remember to use the Campaign Countdown Checklist! It will help ensure you have ample time for planning and implementation.

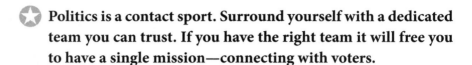 Politics is a contact sport. Surround yourself with a dedicated team you can trust. If you have the right team it will free you to have a single mission—connecting with voters.

FOLLOW THE CAMPAIGN PYRAMID PRINCIPLE

*"There's nothing more important in a campaign
than human contact between a candidate and a voter."*

A MISSED OPPORTUNITY

One year, we observed a local businesswoman running for office for the first time. Early in the campaign, however, she blew a golden opportunity to influence voters and potential contributors. The result? She had to self-fund the majority of her campaign and work much harder to win precious votes.

It was late summer and she was attending a meet-and-greet fundraiser in her honor. The event was packed with influential members of the community who were movers and shakers with the ability to bring the three most critical things to her campaign: influence, money, and votes.

While the guests milled around talking to one another, the candidate did not leave her comfort zone. For much of the event, she stood chatting with her co-workers and family. The evening passed and several guests left the event untouched by her presence. Eventually, she did break out of her comfort zone and worked the crowd that remained, but it was almost too little, too late.

She failed to understand that the opportunity was not in nurturing the guaranteed votes of her inner circle (voters in the top of the pyramid), but in making a strong favorable impression and gaining support from the people who assembled to get to know her. She managed to win the election against a tough opponent, but her path could have been much easier had she applied the *Power of the Pyramid* and the excellent opportunity presented to her early in the race.

You will hear us say over and over that a candidate should never miss a chance to make a personal connection with a voter. A candidate's contact with a voter is an opportunity to turn one vote into many, because that voter you just "touched" could, in turn, talk up your candidacy to his or her friends and family. By making positive contact with 50 people, you may earn yourself several hundred votes. Conversely, a negative interaction can snowball out of control in a hurry. Always be on your game!

Long before you are certain you are going to run for office, you need to take stock of the "influencers" around you. If you are in a position to seriously consider a campaign, you should know the people in your community who supported the current elected officials. *These* are the people you need to have on your side. In a town of 50,000 residents, about 25 people can have enough influence to get someone elected. Seek out the people who you know others look to when considering their vote, such as current and past office holders. These influencers will usually be happy to spend time with you. The more they know about you, the better their opinions will resonate when they talk to others. Make certain you have a solid base of "influencers" on your team, not just individuals who will vote for you.

 The candidate's job is to make contact with voters at every opportunity: one-on-one, small groups, large groups, and everything in between. Attend as many events as possible, and never miss an opportunity to interact with voters.

THE CAMPAIGN PYRAMID PRINCIPLE

Most individuals know that a candidate should have at least some level of interaction with constituents at various points in a campaign. The questions for candidates are, "when and how much?" Some candidates envision themselves standing at a podium addressing hundreds, or thousands, of voters and making *appearances* at fancy fundraising events. Is that what wins votes? In their minds it does, which can cause them to feel they have appropriately covered the *when* and the *how much* of constituent interaction. After the votes come in, they find themselves at a loss for why they were defeated.

Some candidates believe that the biggest war chest wins. We've seen candidates spend and spend only to still lose an election because they didn't know the critical element in capturing people's votes. Still others believe that lots of interaction with the right socialites or supportive elected officials will drive in a majority vote. We have unfortunately seen the bottom fall out of many such campaigns. Yet, time and time again, our simple little secret principle brought victory to our camp.

At this point you may be dying to ask, "What is the Pyramid Principle? And why is it a secret?" The concept is almost too simple, which may be the reason why it seems to be almost unheard of as an actual campaign principle or strategy. We'd like to consider it a secret—a secret weapon, that is. Too often, people fall into the trap of thinking that more complex, more expensive, and more exclusive is better. Celebrity status, popularity, and big bucks win elections. Right? Wrong. Those things win girlfriends and boyfriends. All jokes aside, money, popularity, and status will help a campaign, but following the Pyramid Principle wins elections.

The Pyramid dictates where a candidate's time is spent and, *more importantly,* where it is not spent. The Pyramid Principle sets the stage for the campaign and the focus for each member of the campaign team. We promote this concept as the foundation

★ 15 WAYS TO BEAT YOURSELF IN AN ELECTION

1. Don't follow the Pyramid Principle
2. Don't have a strategy
3. Start the campaign too late
4. Don't use funds wisely
5. Too few team members and volunteers
6. No message or poor message
7. Don't understand local community needs
8. Run a dirty campaign
9. Don't spend the required hours
10. Have low name recognition
11. Weak social media
12. Not enough signs or signs not placed in proper locations
13. Don't obtain endorsements
14. Don't have influencers on your side
15. Lack of personal involvement in the community

for the entire campaign. If you do not learn anything else in this book, you need to know that following the Pyramid Principle will get you more votes than anything else, especially in a local election. Make this principle the cornerstone of your strategy.

What is the secret of a Pyramid Principle campaign? *Strategic Human Contact.* There is nothing more important in a campaign than human contact between a candidate and a voter. With all of the factors in a campaign that are forever changing, the one factor that will never change is the human desire for relationships. The candidate's ability to meet with voters will open doors for gathering information about the concerns and culture of a community. Following the Pyramid Principle will help candidates create levels of trust and familiarity with the

> There is nothing more important in a campaign than human contact between a candidate and a voter.

people they intend to lead—a personal bridge if you will— and personal bridges win votes.

Three Tiers of the Pyramid

The Pyramid Principle consists of three tiers: top, middle, and bottom. Each tier will present its own set of challenges and rewards, but the greatest reward is winning the majority of votes to win the election. The Pyramid illustrates where the candidate's time should be spent, or *not* spent, and gives a visual reminder of where the most votes are located.

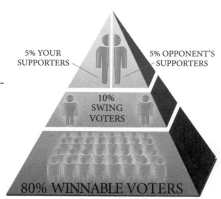

The Top 10

The top of the Pyramid is made up of 10 percent of all voters. It includes family members, co-workers, and friends. We'll call this group the *Guaranteed Votes Club.* This top 10 percent also includes the people who are guaranteed to vote for your opponent. You are going to get one half of the votes in the top of the pyramid, and your opponent is going to get the other half. Pretty easy so far? Good.

Now, get out of the top of the pyramid, slam the door, and never look back. *There is nothing you can do in the top of the pyramid to get votes—and getting votes is what this is all about.*

Your job is to get votes by making personal contact with voters and convincing them to support you, nothing else. You can hang out with your friends and do all that other fun stuff after you win. Keep them involved and energized, but realize you have their vote. It's a done deal. No more selling to them; you would be wasting your time with the wrong people.

 Do not waste your time in the top of the pyramid.

The Middle 10

In the middle of the pyramid are the *Swing Voters.* These are the 10 percent of people whose votes may be influenced by your value system and your message. For the most part, these folks are educated on the issues, keep up on current events, and have more than an average interest in government affairs. Some come to the table with pre-existing partisan allegiances, and others cast their vote because they have an agenda that aligns with one of the candidates. There's not a whole lot of difference between this tier and the top tier if you think about it. A few may be convinced to support you and might even come on your side as they see your campaign unfold. It's nice to have their votes and you should work to get them, but remember they are only 10 percent of the voters. Because they run in civic circles and seem to have influence, candidates tend to spend a lot of time with this group. If you dedicate 100 percent of your time with them, and all the stars line up, you may get a few more votes and some added influence over other voters, which is good. But do the math. In the big picture, this 10 percent is almost insignificant considering the effort required and limited time you have.

The Bottom 80

Now, for the winning strategy: *make the floor of the Pyramid the foundation of your campaign.* There is no need to enter those top two floors of the Pyramid again. You have been there, and for the most part, wasted your time. Hopefully, your competition is up there messing around. The longer he or she stays up there the better.

You should live in the lower part of the Pyramid because that is where the action is. This is where the *Winnable Voters* are. Sound overwhelming? Well, it's not. As a matter of fact, the scope of your campaign efforts just got a lot more focused.

In a recent mayoral race, we watched three well-qualified candidates battle to the end. Any of the three would have been a great mayor, so the choice was not easy. The playing field was virtually level. All three had about the same experience and funding, and all were well thought of in the community.

Two of them used most of the strategies we recommend in this book. It was a close race, but they finished first and second. They entered the race early, worked hard, made lots of personal voter contacts, and made good use of social media. The winner was often seen at two in the morning putting out signs. We don't recommend the candidate being the sign installer, but the scenario shows that dedication and hard work normally ends in victory.

The third candidate provided the key lesson, however. He was predicted to win but lost by a wide margin. He was ill-advised to wait until the last minute to announce that he was in the race. By then, the other two candidates had months of campaigning under their belts with volunteers in place and a voter base established. Some people believed rumors that Candidate Three was not going to run. And because there was no evidence to the contrary, they committed early to one of the other candidates.

Candidate Three had very few signs and less of a social media presence. But more importantly, he was far behind in personal voter contact.

In our view, the loss occurred because Candidate Three depended primarily on several large neighborhoods. Unfortunately for him, there were not enough voters in those neighborhoods. Candidate Three had a sense of having most of the votes in the bag without realizing he was campaigning with his allies in the top two tiers of the Pyramid. He already had most of their votes going in. Meanwhile, Candidates One and Two focused their attention on voters in the bottom 80 percent of the Pyramid.

We can imagine the people in the bottom 80 percent of Candidate Three's voter list screaming, "You'd better give me attention, because come election time my vote counts just as much as anyone else's."

Make the bottom floor of the Pyramid the foundation of your campaign.

Your work as a candidate is where the majority of votes are, that 80 percent. Nowhere else. So get a pair of comfortable shoes and start walking. Don't forget your voter list!

It is worth mentioning that most new candidates make the basic mistake of not understanding the Pyramid Principle, and therefore run around like headless chickens overspending and overworking. In the end, they join that long list of candidates who beat themselves. Yes, they beat themselves. They set out to defeat their opponents, but by adhering to poor campaign decisions and poor use of strategies, they ended up sealing their own fates.

Sometimes even seasoned campaigners take years to figure it out. They spend money like crazy, work hard, take shortcuts, and forever seek the easy way. In doing so, they miss the surest path to the winner's circle.

 The Pyramid Principle concept is not only the least costly of all the strategies out there, it is by far the most effective.

In another example, the perfect candidate ran for sheriff in one of the largest counties in the entire country. He should have won by a landslide. Instead, he was soundly defeated. He was popular, an excellent speaker, and extremely well qualified, with a work history that could not be matched by anyone, anywhere. He had it all, including a war chest of well over $100,000. He also had an army of people behind him, leveraging almost every campaign strategy known to mankind. He stayed close to his friends and co-workers during the campaign. This was a huge mistake. The cold hard fact is, he did not need to spend one second with them. He was already assured of their votes, but staying close to his inner circle was easy, fun, and comfortable. Being so caught up in the glory a campaign can bring, he forgot to do the basics—get people to vote for him. All the window dressing does not bring votes. Touching voters does. It's that simple.

On the other hand, the underdog, with less than $5,000 and just a handful of volunteers, had no choice but to hit the streets and run a grassroots campaign. He was working within the Pyramid Principle and didn't even know it.

THE KEY TO WINNING

Being able to relate to the people who will elect you puts you on the path to win. However, if you don't get anything else from this book, get this: the key to winning the majority of the majority is personal contact, and that trumps all the other campaign strategies and tactics out there. The campaign Pyramid Principle is the foundation of every strategy and tactic found in this book. Will you be able to personally speak to every single voter? Probably not. But through careful planning and execution, there is a way to personally and thoughtfully touch and garner the majority of those 80 percent of winnable voters.

 Knowing who and where the voters are is the path to victory. Your job from now until Election Day is meeting with voters. Get out of your comfort zone and go meet with the 80 percent who will make the difference.

THE INTERVIEW:
WHY THE PYRAMID PRINCIPLE?

WES AND I HAD JUST FINISHED designing signs when, around quitting time, an older model car pulled up to our modest little office. A good-looking young man got out, straightened his tie, and headed for our door.

Wes groaned. "The next president of the United States is arriving." The door squeaked open and our new victim, I mean candidate, walked in.

"Hello, my name is Matt Owens and I want to run for city council. I heard that you guys are the best in the business."*(Wonder where he got that information?)*

"Nice to meet you, Matt," Wes and I said in unison.

I pointed to a chair. "Sit down. I'm still wondering who said good things about us. One does not make a lot of friends in this line of work. Wes can count his on one hand, and I'm not sure if I'm included."

With no experience, no name recognition, and very little money, Matt asked for our help to win a city council seat against a well-known incumbent who had more than 20 years of civic experience. We quickly realized our win percentage was about to take a hit. Normally, this type of dreamer would be lucky to get even his family to vote for him, let alone anyone with a whisper of political interest. Regardless, he was interested in learning more about "the Pyramid Principle" that he had heard about.

"Matt, if you want to hire us we will do our best to ensure you become a city council member. We'll coach you and provide our years of research and experience. You'll benefit most from our knowledge of the best and worst campaign practices. We'll apply what works best and try not to let you repeat others' mistakes. And we'll shadow you from start to finish, ensuring you get the biggest bang for the buck. Speaking of bucks, Matt, do you have any?"

"He's just joking," Wes said as he cut me off. "We'll get into that later, but we are quite reasonable."

Huh? Did he forget the part about us being the best in the business— not to mention our overwhelming win record? I would think that would bring the big bucks.

Matt was anxious to learn about the Pyramid Principle, so we got right into it.

Matt: So, I hear you guys have helped a lot of first-time candidates, like me, win elections?

Wes: We've done pretty well in the past with our candidates, new and experienced. When people follow our Pyramid Strategy, they avoid a lot of campaign blunders, which frees them up to focus on what really works.

Matt: So tell me, what really is the purpose of the Pyramid Principle?

Ron: Well, based on the three-tiered model, our goal is pretty evident. It's connecting with 80 percent of the voting population—those in the widest part of the pyramid—with the candidate's presence and message. You won't be able to affect the other two tiers much and there aren't that many votes to get. Therefore, you don't waste precious time or resources trying to win them.

Matt: Why would a candidate choose the Pyramid Principle rather than some other technique or strategy?

Ron: There are lots of strategies out there, but based on our experience, research, and surveys, there is nothing that pulls votes like Pyramid Principle campaigning because it focuses on getting support from actual voters in an organized way. The candidate gets the biggest return for his or her effort at a very low cost. Although the Pyramid Principle works best in smaller communities, it also works well with other types of campaigns. The idea is to make contact with actual voters. The response we get from citizens is overwhelming when they actually meet the candidate, especially at their homes.

Matt: You mean the candidate is supposed to go to peoples' homes? Isn't that dangerous?

Wes: Of course you go to their homes. The difference is you do it with a well-laid plan to best focus your time and resources.

Ron: Here's the key: The Pyramid Principle pulls votes almost every time. We get very little rejection: not even one half of one percent of the contacts made. There are other benefits too, such as getting homeowners to put up your sign, and some will even donate to your campaign. We've had more than a few who actually joined the campaign team as volunteers. If they meet you and agree to support you, they will tell others, which is where the snowball factor comes in. For example, it is said that placing a sign in someone's yard will bring in at least 5 additional votes from their neighbors. Add another 20 votes if, in turn, they talk to their family and friends. In a sense, they become like salespeople for you. That would likely not happen if they noticed a newspaper ad, attended a public speech, received emails, or all the other things believed to work. We believe the one thing that gets the true support of people, and convinces them to vote for you is contact—especially one-on-one time at their homes. That is what the Power of the Pyramid Principle is about. As we've stated before, and we will again, many candidates take shortcuts using devices such as advertising, which is expensive, with very little return. Our Pyramid Principle concept is strong and we don't mind saying it!

Matt: So, do others also use this strategy?

Ron: A few use the door-to-door contact—the ones we work with for sure and others who copy us—but many do not. If they do, they don't do it well. We've found candidates and campaign teams who are unaware of the *voter contact list* and even fewer who understand the *precinct analysis,* or even know it exists. It is not about just walking around a neighborhood and knocking on doors. You will know exactly which doors to knock on. You will know what addresses to send mailers to. You will know who to call by phone. You will not use the shotgun approach, but will follow an exact plan to get the biggest return.

Matt: Yeah, you'll have to show me those.

Wes: Other well-known strategies, the most effective ones in our opinion, are also in this little book we put together *(Wesley hands Matt a copy of the* Power of the Campaign Pyramid*)*. We discuss a strategy for building the right platform, message points, signs, campaign mailers, and social media strategies, just to name a few. But it still goes back to the least expensive and most effective strategy—person-to-person contact following the voter list after completing a precinct analysis. That's the heart of a campaign based on the Pyramid Principle.

Matt: Wow, I'm seriously impressed. Who would have thought that something so simple could be so . . . so powerful? And there is almost no cost involved. I like that. I'm willing to put in the time. That's what I'm about.

STEP 5
STRATEGIZE TO WIN

"Whoever is first in the field and awaits the coming of the enemy, will be fresh for the fight: whoever is second in the field and has to hasten to battle will arrive exhausted." – SUN TZU

AT THIS POINT, THE BIG PIECES of your campaign puzzle are beginning to fall into place. You've got your winning team, you understand the basics of *Pyramid Principle campaigning,* and now it's time to move forward with a strong platform and a solid strategic plan for taking care of all the essential details.

BE STRATEGIC TO SUCCEED

There's an old saying that if you fail to plan, you plan to fail. Planning a campaign is not much different from developing a business or marketing plan. Your campaign manager, A-Team, and you, will set your strategy and establish time lines. Take your time and do it right the first time—a well-thought-out plan will pay big dividends later. Starting early allows you to test and adjust the plan quietly, behind the scenes. Marketing people know that you never bring out a new product all at once. Test small, test fast, and fail early. This gives you time to adjust and fine tune your strategy. The same principle applies in a campaign. *Measure twice and cut once.*

A victory is the sum of many small things done well. We have seen campaign teams fall into chaos because they didn't plan ahead and failed to take care of all the little things that should have been done much earlier in the process. Here is one scenario that we've seen too many times. The "fail-to-plan team" is out in the field campaigning when suddenly they realize they don't have signs. The team frantically tries to call in a last-minute sign order only to learn that there is a long waiting list. Campaign season is in full swing, but this team is left hanging out to dry. Would that little campaign countdown checklist have helped? We know so.

There are many pieces to the puzzle, and almost every one of them can be in place before the show goes live. We'll say it again. Have your campaign manager and A-Team in place months in advance. Designate people to tasks, set deadlines, and follow up to be sure it gets done—use the checklist! By doing so, the little failures will be few and far between.

THE MESSAGE

One of the first tasks to tackle is developing your campaign platform and message. This requires a great deal of research and strategic thinking, so start early and rely on all the talents of your campaign manager and other A-Team members.

Determine the Campaign Focus

Determining the right focus is a critical element of a candidate's campaign. The task here is to determine the relevant issues, establish a platform, and create talking points and stump speeches that will resonate with voters and persuade them to vote for you. It will not matter how hard you work or how loudly you speak if your message does not connect with the wants and needs of the voters.

Research the Issues
Some issues aren't difficult to research because they are on the front page of the newspaper. Talking with citizens provides insight to a long list of other issues that may never reach the media until they get political traction. What are the major issues in your district? Are they new or recurring? And just who is affected by these issues? Another underlying question is, why do these issues exist and why are they not resolved? Having the answers to these questions will not only help you plan your focus, but move you well on your way to developing solid solutions.

The one thing you don't want to do is promise something that you cannot deliver. Keep in mind, you are just one of the many people that it takes to accomplish change. You can't do anything on your own. As an office holder, your job is to sell ideas to others. It is tempting to make spur-of-the-moment promises, but be careful: voters remember, keep score, and will hold you accountable. Sometimes candidates are talking when they should be listening.

Prioritize the issues list

From the list of issues researched, it is important to prioritize them based on a number of factors:

- Voters' needs and interests.
- Which issues you will (and won't) have authority over when you win office.
- What the issue represents.
- What you can reasonably accomplish.
- Your level of belief or passion for the issue.

You may not be able to address all of the issues, but you must be able to effectively handle two or three.

Create Your Platform

With a good grasp of the issues, it's time to create your platform. Voters want to know at least two things about you: why you are running and what you plan to do if elected. A platform is a series of positions on various political issues that promote a candidate. Look at a platform as your stage and you are the star of the show. You have the microphone and this is your chance to tell the voters who you are and what you plan to do that will make their lives better.

You will want to identify issues that are specific to your community. It is not surprising that over 60 percent of the voters surveyed stated that the *platform message* was the most important item that swayed their vote.

- Know, in priority order, what the most important issues are to the majority of voters.
- Know which issues you can be sincerely passionate about.

59

- Become a subject matter expert on the ones you choose.
- Be well versed on ALL of the top issues.

You should have two or three high-impact message points that will resonate with the majority of the voters. Your message points will be on your campaign material, presented through your social media, in your press releases, and you will constantly beat the drum with them. People want to hear about issues and solutions that directly involve them, but you need to be specific on your main messages. Voters need to know why you are the better candidate, and how you will address their concerns. Look at what the other candidates are talking about. If there is a consensus, you may want to align with them. You and your team need to do your homework and get this one right. Your platform and how you sell your message is a key make-or-break point in your campaign.

Wrong Focus, Exit Stage Right
We once had a person come to us who wanted to run for city council. My first question, "Why?" was aimed at eliciting his platform. His answer was, "The biggest problems in our city are the traffic on the freeway and the problems in our school system." I reminded him that the city has no control over either issue. Here was a decent man who wanted to improve his community. But his message was way off. It was apparent that he didn't do his homework as he lost the race by the largest margin in the city's history.

Craft Your Talking Points
After having done your homework on the issues and getting input from your campaign team and other knowledgeable people on local affairs, you should decide which issues you want to champion.

Focus on two or three strong, hard-hitting talking points. Our survey showed that the candidate's message has a very strong influence on how 63 percent of our respondents will vote. Your message must come from the heart, and even more important, be factual and truthful. Do your homework and make sure your statements are bulletproof. You must believe in your messages, not waiver, and be comfortable and confident in selling it. It is a good idea to get input from others. Communicate your message in a memorable way. Be specific, and always be prepared to defend your positions. How are you going to do that? Why? When? What will the results be? How do you know? Do you have the power and authority to do it? All of this must be explained in the simplest terms to a wide range of audiences. Which leads us to the stump speech.

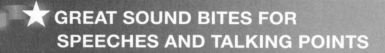

★ GREAT SOUND BITES FOR SPEECHES AND TALKING POINTS

"...Safer neighborhoods and safer cities."

"I will work closely with our police department and court system to make sure crime prevention is on top of their priority list."

"This city must have a zero tolerance policy when it comes to crime."

"Nothing would make me happier than to put the word on the street that our city is a place criminals don't want to be."

 You can always mix in a few feel-good ideas such as quality of life, safer neighborhoods, better streets, more parks....

Stump Speeches

From your two or three talking points, you will need to create one-minute and five-minute stump speeches for any planned or impromptu speaking opportunities. Your stump speech will be used throughout the campaign, with only minor tweaks to appropriately address different audiences that may have different needs.

We all know that a short speech is the best speech. And never exaggerate or lie! Tell voters what you stand for and what you plan to do that will make their lives better. Say it the way you feel it. High energy in small doses works wonders, whether in a comment or in written material.

★ STUMP SPEECH RULES

1. Use them as the situation requires.
2. Stay on message and don't ramble or pontificate.
3. Don't talk like a politician.
4. Know your audience and know how to relate to them. (Don't talk about urban issues to farmers.)
5. Know your strengths and speak of them often.
6. Be honest and direct with your messages.
7. Keep it short, no more than 3 to 5 minutes. Leave them wanting more, not wishing you'd stop talking.

Your Message, Your Passion

Your talking points will become your passion. Get them right. Sound bites work well with the media; they work even better in debates, in speeches, and on social media. Most people will respond to what they value and will appreciate it deeply when it comes from the heart. Here are just a few examples of talking points candidates have used that resonated well with voters:

We are at a crossroads. I am committed to moving this city forward with safer streets, more parks, and riding trails. It takes money and I will support businesses to help us fund our needs in the city. I will never sacrifice our rural culture. We can and must have both.

I am committed to turning our downtown area into a lively, beautiful walking-type village.

I am committed to protecting our rural culture.

I will work to create a business-friendly environment to ensure our status as a self-sufficient city.

I will work to implement safeguards to ensure that we make sound financial decisions.

I will make our community safer.

Traffic congestion within the city will be one of my first priorities.

You get the idea, but you will have to develop your own messages that are unique to your community.

Taxes—The Kiss of Death

If you say anything that will raise individual taxes you are toast. You may be right in what you believe, and some people will even understand that to improve services requires funding, and that may have to come in the form of higher taxes. You are standing in quicksand on funding issues. Say anything that even hints that you are in favor of raising someone's personal taxes and you will sink. Be well prepared for the question, "How do you plan to pay for all these great things you are talking about?" The wrong answer is any statement that hints at raising taxes. Role-play these type of questions with your campaign manager and A-Team to come up with the correct answers. You must be prepared for the tough questions from the public and media. You will get them often. Do your homework and be ready for any possible question that may come up.

Calm Voters' Fears

People sometimes worry that a candidate may have a personal agenda, or will favor certain factions. You can calm those fears with a simple, forthright statement. The two examples below may ease suspicious minds. Personalize them to fit your talking style. Be humble and remember your message is about the voters, not about you. If it comes from the heart, it needs to be said.

- *If I am fortunate enough to earn your vote, I pledge that I will vote for issues that represent the needs and welfare of our entire community. I will never vote for my personal pet projects. I respect the citizens of this great city. I do not believe that I know more than the people I represent. I am human and my faith reminds me that none are perfect and all have fallen short. I will make mistakes, but I also will learn from them and am not afraid to admit errors.*

- *I will never vote in favor of a particular group of people. I want it understood that if I take office I am free of any*

> **Your talking points will become your passion.**

"deals," *promises, or commitments to any individual or groups of people.*

THE ESSENTIALS

As we said, winning a campaign means doing many little things well. Let's go through the whole laundry list. It will help you anticipate every step of the campaign process. Again, take care of these details early, and stay on top of any ongoing tasks.

Getting on the Ballot

There could potentially be a lot more competition on the election field, but sadly, a few people actually miss their qualifying dates or don't complete qualification forms correctly, thus eliminating them from the race before it even gets started. *Don't let it be you.* Research all requirements early, plan early, and implement on time.

As soon as you decide that you are going to run for office, months ahead of election season, your job is to find out how to get this party started and make it work to your advantage. For starters, visit the website of whoever oversees the election process of the position for which you plan to run. It may be the city office, county election board, or the secretary of state. Most will have all the proper forms, affidavits, and training materials located on their website. If you cannot find what you need online, contact the appropriate office by phone or email for a copy of the charter, election laws, and required forms. Do not guess—*know.*

Pointers for Getting Your Name on the Ballot
- Know your dates for qualifying. Most qualifying dates have a window of about a week, but this may vary across regions.

- Know the local election laws and regulations of registering.
- The candidate will be disqualified if the process and paperwork are not completed accurately and on time.
- If you are qualifying by nominating petition, make sure the names you collect are of registered voters and that the names are written legibly.
- Always double check your paperwork to ensure it is accurate and that you are in compliance with all qualifying requirements.

Finally, verify that your opponent has submitted all the correct paperwork in a timely matter. Are they in compliance? Keep in mind that if your opponent is out of compliance it will be a lot easier and cheaper to run unopposed. They will certainly be checking your information to verify your compliance.

How Much: The Financial Plan and Budget

Finances can often determine the power of a campaign. The financial plan will allow you to manage cash flow so that you have funds when you need them the most. It includes the general budget, financial disclosure forms, dates and reports, fundraising goals and major events, donations received, expenditures, and any loans received by the campaign.

Setting your budget is critical to determine how much money your campaign will have to raise. Depending on their strategy, different campaigns may vary regarding budget allocation. However, as a rule of thumb in most local campaigns, spending looks similar to the following:

- 40 percent - Direct Mail
- 40 percent - Marketing (signs, social media, traditional media, handouts, etc.)
- 10 percent - Polling
- 10 percent - Consulting (campaign manager)

Now throw in another 30 percent—for all that unplanned stuff, mistakes, failure to follow the directions in this book, and last-minute panic spending. (I think most campaign veterans will agree.) Consider mapping out three budgets: low, middle, and high. The low budget should represent the least amount of money you need to run the campaign. The middle budget is your best estimate of what you will actually be able to raise. The high budget is what you can spend if your fundraising exceeds your expectations. Plan for all three and then adjust to match your actual fundraising numbers.

Endorsements and Influencers

Key endorsements can be powerful for any campaign. However, you do not want an endorsement that will hurt your campaign. Before you consider endorsements, make sure you complete a risk assessment.

Gather your endorsements early, but release them strategically throughout the campaign to show momentum. Use personal postcards, emails, phone calls, and meet-and-greets to leverage endorsements. Let your endorsers go to work. Ask them to contact their friends to sup-

> ★ **ENDORSEMENT RISK ASSESSMENT**
> 1. Does the endorsement help or hurt the campaign?
> 2. Does the endorsement add value?
> 3. Does the endorser have a hidden agenda? (clue: *I will endorse you if you do this for me.*)

port you not only on Election Day, but in things like fundraising and volunteering. They may help by joining your campaign team and bringing other influential people to it.

Most of the time these people run in the right circles, and they can greatly enhance your chances of victory. There are a few people who can bring numerous votes to a candidate because they are so well connected and trusted. Many people rely on them and ask, "I don't know much about who is running. Who should I vote for?" Just having their name associated with your campaign brings votes. The candidate has little to do with influencing the people who may not vote at all because those people really aren't at all concerned about who gets elected until that trusted person (influencer) contacts them and asks for their support.

Every year we get numerous calls from people asking, "Who should

I vote for?" In a recent city election, we called a friend who is very popular in the real estate world and asked for his help. Even though he did not live in the city and was not eligible to vote in the election, he sent out emails to more than 500 local real estate people and asked them to vote for our candidate. He also asked them to forward his email to their email contacts. We provided a few key message points and he reported that most responded and said they would help. Not necessarily because they knew our candidate, but because they respected and liked the person who asked for their help. Friends asking friends for support is just another attribute of the Pyramid Principle. Personal contact during the campaign can take many forms. Don't just concentrate on your local city or district. Like the real estate person, many did not vote in our city, but they knew people in the city, and in turn they contacted them. There are many ways to skin a cat.

Procuring vs. Securing

We all know the old adages about the "best-laid plans" and "Murphy's Law." One of our clients took a hard blow when, all of a sudden, key endorsers pulled out at the eleventh hour. The strategy was set, and key endorsements, which were sought and secured, would soon be released throughout the campaign to show momentum. At least we *thought* they were secured, until we got the almost fatal news. Almost all of the key endorsers had conspired and released a joint endorsement for our candidate's opponent. Talk about getting hit by lightning! The endorsements were planned to be our road to success, but when that news hit we instantly had turmoil in our man's camp. After wiping off the blood, we re-focused on the initial strategy. Our team was wounded but more determined than ever. We stayed focused on our initial plan, didn't panic, (I think the shock deterred the panic), and once again, the long shot finished first. We learned there is a big difference between "procuring" and "securing" an endorsement. Constant communication and keeping everyone involved and updated is an absolute must. Don't take anyone, especially your influencers, for granted, and keep in mind that your opposition is working hard to steal your supporters. You would take every opportunity to sway your opponents' supporters and convert them to your own, right? Keep your eyes and ears open.

Early Voting

Precincts around the country report that 30 percent of the voters take advantage of the early voting option, with 25 percent voting in person and another 5 percent mailing in absentee ballots. Early voting has increased every year, and the trends show it will continue to grow. Think about that. A third of the votes are in, weeks before Election Day. Just in case that number didn't hit you hard enough, it's worth repeating. *Thirty percent of the voting is done before Election Day.*

That is one more reason to start your campaign early. Pursuing early and absentee voters is a great way to establish an early lead. Pursuing absentee voters is a strategy all its own and should not be taken lightly. Know who these voters are. Contact them early. Think of students away at college, people in the military, people living in a foreign country, or families on vacation, to name a few. Explain to these voters how to obtain absentee ballots and how to vote early if they happen to be in town. There are a ton of votes there, so make the effort to get them. Start with your own campaign team and their network of family and friends. When the time comes, put on a special push to win the early voters. Treat it like the week before Election Day. Get that email blast going, use social media, get the volunteers out posting and waving signs at voting precincts (if allowed), and activate the phone calls.

> Pursuing early and absentee voters is a great way to establish an early lead.

Research Your Opponents

Knowing your opponent can give you a distinct advantage, whether or not that knowledge is used overtly in the campaign. Research can include residency, financial disclosures, voting history, education, and business background, to mention just a few. It may also include areas he or she has focused on in the past or plans to focus on during this campaign. Better do your homework because they are doing theirs on you. If your opponent is an incumbent, know their voting history and any unpopular issues they may have supported. A few reminders here and there will trigger the voters' memory.

A Case in Point: Political Chess
A candidate—we'll call him Mr. Bishop—with impressive credentials ran for judge in a county that is more than 90 percent Republican. His opponent—Mr. Knight—brought almost nothing to the table and was virtually invisible during the campaign. Not a website, not a single sign.

Bishop looked sure to win. Knight's campaign team, however, had uncovered some damaging information. This "dirt" was a back breaker and Knight's team knew it. They kept the information close to the vest. *(Never show your cards too early. Timing is everything. Hold the heavy artillery until the last. Don't allow your opponent time to regroup and react.)* If the news got out, the frontrunner's team would do damage control and try to reposition their candidate. Other candidates might even jump into the race. So Knight's team waited until the campaigns were in their final hours. At the right moment, they leaked the news—Bishop, running as a Republican, had voted Democrat in the past three elections. Checkmate! Game over. Knight, who was out of the country on vacation, was shocked to learn he had won by a landslide.

⭐ **Reminder: Use the Campaign Countdown Checklist.**

You're taking care of all the essential logistics for launching your campaign, and the big day is fast approaching when you will publicly announce your candidacy. By now, checking the steps on your campaign countdown checklist (see pages 14 and 15) should be a well-developed habit. If you think your schedule has been busy, just wait—the pace is about to pick up. So give yourself a reminder to chart your progress through the campaign checklist, and refer back to it often.

STEP 6
START MARKETING

GO TRADITIONAL

*"Almost everything you do in a campaign
is tied to positive, upbeat communication."*

Sign Wars

Okay, we finally got around to it. It is true that some believe whoever wins the sign war wins the election. There's no way to know, but they do bring the show to a level where everyone likes to play. There is more talk about signs and the theft of signs than anything else in a campaign. It has a life of its own, so we need to address it.

It's like cutting the ribbon to officially open election season when the signs pop up like flowers. The first few days are like an art contest. But

© Harperdrewart | Dreamtime.com

71

as the election progresses and more signs are added, the signs just seem to blend into their surroundings. Don't become part of the crowd, and don't waste your time and money becoming part of the clutter.

It takes little talent but a whole army to plant these things. Is it even worth it? We wish the answer could be no. Most people say they hate the signs because they are an eyesore. We agree, but signs do hit the voter mass in a hurry and they are a constant reminder that your candidate is a player. Half of the people surveyed say signs have very little influence on the way they vote. If you read between the lines, then the other half of people surveyed must admit that signs do have some influence.

Signs are more about getting people to vote than anything else. When placed in areas where you have strong support, they will increase the number of citizens who will vote for you.

Signs along right-of-ways are often a blur of color to drivers passing by at 30 to 40 miles per hour. It is much better to have ONE large sign (generally 6x4 feet) than five of the small signs (24x18 inches) that blend in with every other candidate's signs running for office. The larger signs will likely require a permit from the city. They may not be cheap, but placed in strategic, high-volume locations they will do MUCH

★ SIGN DON'TS

- Don't allow your sign army to be too aggressive.

- Don't install signs for the sake of getting rid of them. A sign in the wrong person's yard could present you in the wrong light by association. (For example, giving a sign to someone who is not well thought of in the neighborhood or in the city.)

- Don't get caught up in a "sign war"! It is nothing but a distraction.

more for you than small signs in a blur of red, white, and blue.

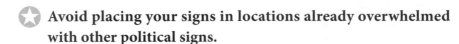 **Avoid placing your signs in locations already overwhelmed with other political signs.**

Sign Power!

When you walk the neighborhoods and it feels like the homeowner is willing to help you, ask for three things: 1) their vote, 2) permission to put a sign in their yard, and 3) funding. If they agree to put a sign in their yard, your driver and volunteers will do that on the spot as you move to the next house. (It is a good practice to place your signs in planted areas, pine straw islands or areas with no grass, rather than in areas that will be mowed). A yard sign virtually locks in the homeowner's support, but more importantly, it sends a signal to others in the neighborhood. It is said that one sign in a yard brings at least five votes. Use your website, email blasts, mailers, and other means to make it simple to request a sign. Your sign people need to be fed the requests as soon as possible and get the signs installed within 24 hours. They should make contact with the homeowner who requested the sign to ensure it is placed where they want it.

Signs are necessary, but they do not win elections. Remember: less is more. A dozen well-placed large signs will have more impact than hundreds of small signs thrown out at random.

Now that we have determined that playing the sign game is a necessary part of a campaign, is there a strategy for signs? You'd better believe it. There is a right way and a wrong way to manage signs. For simplicity's sake we are going to list them in no particular order.

Sign Suggestions

1. Big signs are better than small ones. Check with local regulations as they may require a special permit and there could be size restrictions.
2. Do not place small yard signs one behind the other. Instead, install three signs side by side. This will give the same effect as a larger sign and will overwhelm other signs.
3. Keep your signs simple. People speeding by in cars will give it a quick glance at best. They will see your name and that's about it.
4. Never date a sign. People know when the election is and you may want to use the signs in the next election.
5. We recommend signs with two contrasting colors (white does not count) that have strong visual appeal. Forget the stars and stripes and all the window dressing. The first name should be small and the

last name should be in large bold letters and almost fill the entire sign. Also include the office your are running for. That's it. Nothing else.

6. Know the city, county, and state ordinances regarding sign locations, sizes allowed, etc. There are many. The sign police will take your signs if they don't meet code or are placed in unauthorized areas.

7. Location is critical. Think of high-traffic roads, intersections, and around office buildings and businesses. The window of a business is highly effective; it tells their customers that you have their support.

8. A few days before elections you will see people waving signs near major roads and intersections. Make your signs stand out by putting them on top of 8-foot poles. They will be seen above all others.

9. Lawn signs are a great way to increase name recognition and get votes. The number of signs does not necessarily equal votes. It's about location, location, location.

10. Place signs in yards that are at the entry of a neighborhood. People will see them several times a day as they go in and out. If you can put them on the lawns of the homeowners association officers or other well-known people, that is a plus.

11. Previous office holders who support you will likely have a list of where they placed signs; ask them to introduce you to the homeowners who displayed their signs.

12. Signs too close to the street or median are normally against local codes and are often confiscated by local authorities.
13. The most commonly used size is the 18x24-inch yard sign with metal brackets. Metal brackets are highly recommended and much easier to install.
14. Volume and off-season buying brings discounts.
15. Regularly check on your placed signs. Some will come up missing, so be prepared to replace them quickly.

The night before Election Day, your sign people should be prepared to pick up all the yard signs in neighborhoods and get them reinstalled at roads leading to the polling locations. And, of course, they should recover them and all the remaining signs that were put out and store them when the election is over so they can be used again in the next campaign. Leaving signs out long after the election is over creates a poor image for the candidate.

Never touch your opponents' signs. It is against the law and you will likely go to jail. If you or anyone on your team is caught even touching your opponents' signs, your campaign is over. If we ever found out that a member of our team was stealing, moving, or tampering with the opponents' signs, we would resign as consultants. We tell everyone involved with our campaigns it will not be tolerated in any way, shape, or form, and we will be the first one to call the police on them. No doubt, people will steal your signs. So be it. Don't stoop to their level. Take the high road.

Magnets, Decals, Billboards

Magnets and decals on vehicles are like mobile billboards. Speaking of billboards, if your city allows them, by all means, reserve them early and use them. They are hard to beat and provide much more value than hundreds of other signs.

Giveaways
Be careful not to get carried away here. Think of just one or two

significant items. July 4th is known for parades, campaigns, and hot weather. Imagine hundreds of people fanning themselves with a handheld fan with a picture of you on it. Another item could be a refrigerator magnet with important numbers on it, such as: emergency numbers, power company, poison control, cable company, and, of course, your picture with your phone number. Think of things that people will actually use and keep. The rest of the junk normally finds its way to the garbage can.

Automated Calls

An interesting aspect of automated calls is that the candidate who places the most automatic calls usually wins. Although 83 percent of voters in our survey stated that automated calls are annoying and did not influence their votes, the fact is, they are very effective. A very short, personalized message works well, and a call from the candidate or candidate's spouse, a celebrity, or someone who is well known in the community has a good chance of being listened to. Come up with a great attention getter that will be heard in the first three seconds.

Phone Banks

The size of your budget and volunteer team will dictate when you start phone bank calls. Each experienced phone bank volunteer can dial an average of 20 numbers per hour—about double the number of doors you can knock on in the same amount of time. You can also do phone bank calls regardless of the weather. At worst, have your phone bank up and running no later than the week prior to Election Day.

Important Phone Bank Procedures—Part 1
- Make it fun. (Maybe include a few pizza parties.)
- Email volunteers in advance of the phone bank.
- Ask volunteers to bring a cell phone, charger, and a list of names and phone numbers of people they know in the voting district.
- Have each volunteer call his or her personal contact list first. These calls are quick and easy. Ask for their vote and move on.

Next comes the more difficult part: calling people on the voter list who aren't known by your volunteers. Every voter needs a call—have that voter history list available.

Phone Bank Procedures—Part 2
Divide the phone lists up by teams, each with a captain.

The phone bank captain:
- Reads aloud the names from the voter list to volunteers.
- Assigns phone calls to volunteers as they acknowledge people they are acquainted with.
- Crosses off assigned names and continues the process.
- Assigns phone calls to voters not known by anyone.

After a few calls it will become easier. Don't be concerned with a little rejection here and there. Expect to be hung up on; don't take it personally. A very short script may help. But don't read from it. When calling unfamiliar people, callers should try to find common ground and personalize the call. As you can see, this is a big task and may take several days. Use the candidate and his or her family as well. Their calls will almost always get a better response.

These calls bring more votes than you can imagine, especially if the caller and receiver know each other. This is the Pyramid Principle at work: a friend asking a friend for a favor, in this case, "Please vote for my candidate." Do not criticize your competitor, and keep the calls short. Always ask for their votes. If you run out of time or volunteers, consider a professional phone banking team. They are effective and reasonably priced.

Direct Mail

A majority of your mailing lists will be pulled from the voters' history database. Of those we surveyed, 76 percent said the message on the direct mail pieces strongly influenced them. Keep mail pieces simple and personable. This is not the time to tell your life story. At best, people will look at the picture and a couple of key message points. The reader's

attention span is from the mailbox to the wastepaper basket. Remember, you want high-energy messages in small doses.

The above example gives a short, strong message. As you look at it, ask yourself what hits the subconscious. Can you find it? It is the teddy bear. Look again. The message hits you, the children make you feel good, but the teddy bear hits the heart. The same goes with other feel-good mailers. Clever quotes with pictures of families, children, and pets always seem to work. If voters relate to you, their memories will be triggered on Election Day. Issues and all the political hype do not mean much to many voters.

Three Direct Mail Pieces You Must Send

At least three mail pieces should be sent to likely voters. Direct mail is one of the most expensive parts of a campaign, so you need to target the voters from your voter list. This is just one example where analyzing the voter file early really pays off.

The first direct mail piece is an introduction with your message. The second piece will show a comparison between the candidates (see next page). The third piece should be a short feel-good message encouraging people to vote for you, such as the example above.

Compare the Candidates	Matt	Smith
Supports **protecting** our rural look and feel	✓	✓
Fought AGAINST fire station and police station at Birmingham Crossroads		✓
Fought AGAINST 206 acre Birmingham Park		✓
Believes that homeowners should foot 86% of Milton's tax bill		✓
Does **NOT** believe Milton is in competition with surrounding areas for revenues		✓
IGNORED potential conflicts of interest by voting against business license applications from competitors to her family business		✓
FALSELY claimed ▓▓▓▓▓ endorsed her campaign		✓
Supports **creating** neighborhood parks	✓	
Promotes trail systems and adaptive parks **NOW**	✓	
Backs funding for public horse trails	✓	
Champions right of communities to make decisions for safer roads for families and young drivers	✓	
Supports measures to lower the homeowner tax burden	✓	
Favors measures that will increase our property values	✓	

ATLANTA CONSTITUTION JOURNAL

SOME IN NORTH FULTON FEAR NEW FACILITY

Craig Schneider July 7, 1998

Some People see a planned fire station, police station and park in northwest Fulton County as a boon, while others in the Birmingham community say it will be a curse... "It's a blessing," said Peggy Kelly of the planned public safety station. and park. "With the fire department there, it won't take them all evening to get here." "We want to minimize development," said Julie Smith...

On Nov. 8 - The right choice for Our future is Matt Owens.

Please vote on or before Nov. 8, 2011
Matt Owens, Candidate for Your Area
www.matt4u.com

Have the last mail piece arrive as close to the day before the election as possible so your opposition does not have time to react and counter your message. Keep in mind that the U.S. Postal Service asks that they receive all bulk mail AT LEAST six to seven days before Election Day. This means that your design should be complete at least two weeks before then so you can get the piece printed, addressed, and in the mail on time. There are few things worse than a great piece arriving after the election. If you can afford it, send mail to voters who do not usually vote but live in areas with high voter turnout. NEVER send mailers to a non-registered voter. But do remember those early voters. They're 30 percent of the turnout, and growing.

Postcards

Postcards are a very cost-effective way to get your message out. There is something about a postcard that makes it seem personal and important. A nice picture on it will add to the reader's curiosity. Again, *high energy in small doses* works best. Three or four sentences in large font are the most effective. Postcards should be customized with an appealing message and sent to selected groups. For example, a postcard sent to a

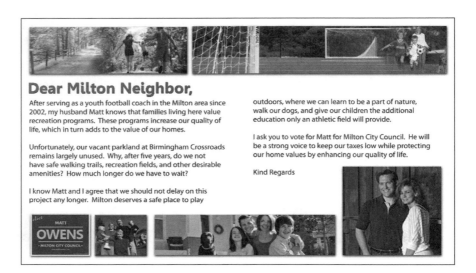

Dear Milton Neighbor,

After serving as a youth football coach in the Milton area since 2002, my husband Matt knows that families living here value recreation programs. These programs increase our quality of life, which in turn adds to the value of our homes.

Unfortunately, our vacant parkland at Birmingham Crossroads remains largely unused. Why, after five years, do we not have safe walking trails, recreation fields, and other desirable amenities? How much longer do we have to wait?

I know Matt and I agree that we should not delay on this project any longer. Milton deserves a safe place to play

outdoors, where we can learn to be a part of nature, walk our dogs, and give our children the additional education only an athletic field will provide.

I ask you to vote for Matt for Milton City Council. He will be a strong voice to keep our taxes low while protecting our home values by enhancing our quality of life.

Kind Regards

elect
MATT
OWENS
- MILTON CITY COUNCIL -

business would have a different message than one sent to a residence.

Specialized groups vote and can be loyal supporters if you can find common ground with them. Let's say you're a veteran and you send a postcard to all the veterans and people with sons and daughters in the military. That, my friend, is a bunch of guaranteed votes. Think they will tell others? You'd better believe it. Another great example of this strategy is to put together a unique message to retirees. Your message should resonate well with the masses, but a special postcard to retirees might have a message just for them.

How about a road improvement message for select neighborhoods? An emphasis on lower taxes through the Homestead Exemption? For soccer moms, talk about more playgrounds, parks, and recreation facilities. The list is endless, but be careful you aren't seen as someone who is all things to all people just to get their votes.

Dear fellow business owners,

I am not one to sugar coat anything and prefer to say it the way it is. After years of bad experiences and lip service from --------------- Milton City Council Member, we have an opportunity for change.

She has been an anchor around the necks of Milton businesses for years and will continue to stymie us at every opportunity.

Her opponent, Matt Owens, appreciates the value of Milton businesses. He understands business and what it takes to be successful. He will be a loud, strong voice on behalf of business people as the replacement for the anti-business council person we have had to tolerate for too long.

Please encourage all you know to vote for Matt Owens this coming Tues. Nov. 8. It will be a vote for your future. Let's sink the anchor.

As often as possible, have the postcards sent to the respective groups from someone they know and respect. The neighborhood team leader may want to personalize the message to appeal to his or her neighborhood and sign it.

Door Hangers/ Door-to-Door Contact

If there is any tactic that is worth more than the price of gold, it is door-to-door contact. Remember the teachings of the Pyramid Principle: live with the 80 percent, and, of that group, contact those on the current voter list. Going door to door helps build the personal contacts that are essential for you or your team to meet with your

> Nearly 70 percent of voters polled…said that meeting the candidate in person at their home strongly influenced their vote.

constituency. *If your time is limited,* target the largest neighborhoods in your community that voted in the last election. That one personal contact with a voter will leave a lasting impression. If the people are not

home, be sure to leave a door hanger. Pre-sign it with a personalized note saying you are sorry you missed them but would appreciate their vote. The door hanger will have your message points and your phone number with a request to call you if they would like to talk to you about anything at all. Nearly 70 percent of voters polled in our survey said that meeting the candidate in person at their home strongly influenced their vote.

Name (Tag) Recognition

To help voters remember you, create a positive, consistent, and recognizable personal image. For example, develop a color theme for your campaign. Use it consistently on your signs, mailers, banners, door hangers, push cards, and your name tag.

Speaking of name tags, a large name tag is best, with your first name in small letters and your last name covering most of it (just like your signs). Don't leave home without it. Have several made. Make sure your spouse wears one throughout the campaign as well. One of our advisors must have asked our candidate Matt on 20 different occasions the whereabouts of his name tag. Was it in his car, in his pocket, or on his dresser? We can only say, "Duh," at this point. Each time you find your candidate without his name tag, make him contribute $5.00 to the campaign; no exceptions, and no excuses.

Push Cards

Push cards are information cards you hand out to people one-on-one and at public events. It's like handing out your candidate's business card. Like campaign mailers, push cards should be simple. Don't cover them with lots of words. People won't bother reading them. A nice picture of you with your family and a couple of key message points will do it. You and your team should have an ample supply and hand them out wherever and whenever possible. (See example on next page.)

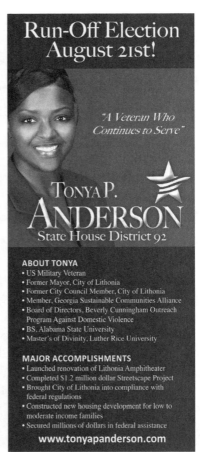

Newspaper Ads

Newspaper ads are expensive, are easily swallowed in a sea of political ads, and most likely won't be noticed by voters. If you have limited funds, you are better off using that money for other things such as mailers. Instead of running ads, your marketing manager should inundate the media with press releases. You never know when reporters need fillers. Encourage a short question-and-answer article. Write opinion editorials to newspapers. There is no cost involved. This is called "earned media." Earned media carries credibility and will make you look stately and knowledgeable. That is much better than a costly political ad.

Get in the Public Eye

Whenever the candidate makes a formal public appearance, and any time the media might show up, have a current press release in your pocket and hand it to reporters. (They love it, and it makes their job easier.) It should relate to the event and support what you say, whether you give a formal speech or a brief comment. Anything positive you can get the media to report is a good thing. If you see a camera, get in front of it. Go where the media goes, and make sure they know you are there.

One of our opposing candidates was a master at this. He was in the paper often. He had pictures taken with firefighters in front of a fire truck, which he used in a variety of ways. He did the same thing with Boy Scouts and VIPs. He tried to give the impression they all supported him. It probably was effective. However, you should assess your actions. Don't be viewed as being too opportunistic or a publicity vulture. Photo ops can give the impression that organizations or individuals support you, but make darn sure they actually do. Call it what you want, but deceit and dishonesty go hand in hand and can pierce your image.

Be a Humble Volunteer Yourself

Don't forget those charity events. Volunteer and get your hands dirty. Take the hard jobs. You will be noticed for it. Of course you should do it for the right reason, which is helping others. At the same time it's a great marketing opportunity because you'll be in contact with the media and voters. Once a year, in a nearby city, there is a large event with more than 10,000 local people attending. At the front gate a couple of local office holders sell tickets. I once asked them, "Why do you stand out there for 8 hours in all kinds of weather?" Their answer: "Where else can I meet so many local citizens in such an informal and fun atmosphere? It gives me a chance to talk to people I don't often see, and I meet hundreds of people for the first time. I wear my name tag, and it attracts people so I get a chance to talk to them." Smart candidates use every opportunity to make positive contacts and build relationships. People remember the officials they meet and talk to. By now you can see that all of these different tactics blend into the Pyramid Principle. Far more than just knocking on doors, the Pyramid is about connecting one-on-one with as many voters as possible.

A long time ago, I was told that if you shake someone's hand and talk to them one-on-one, you'll have a 70 percent chance of getting their support. Even in a small group setting or by phone, your chance of winning their support rises. That surely indicates personal contact works better than all the other tactics out there. Most time-worn campaign strategies work to some degree. But do the math: you have only so much time and so many resources. Where do you want to spend them to assure yourself you get the most votes? Following the Pyramid Principle is the answer.

Radio and TV

Radio and TV advertisements can be very expensive and are sometimes overkill, especially for local elections. The best way to use radio and TV advertising is to get free exposure through media releases and by building relationships with reporters. If you spend time talking with reporters they will contact you when an issue arises or a news story is about to break.

There was a big push in our area to remove the toll from a toll road that has been in place longer than it was mandated. When the topic came up in the media there was no one better to speak with than a person running for political office. The reporters called, and our client got free exposure on his position simply because of the relationship he had with the local media. I don't think it is any secret that the media has a heavy influence on the outcome of an election.

You may want to advertise on the radio. If so, it is important to target your audience and advertise only on the stations with significant listenership in your area. A 30-second message consists of approximately 80 words. Make it memorable and consistent. This is where the audience matches a name with a message. Matt Owens is the "higher property value, lower tax guy." Mention your name at least three times in the message to gain name recognition. The marketing professionals at the radio station will help you refine your message and connect with your target audience. Radio stations will often negotiate their rates.

GO DIGITAL

*"When I took office, only high-energy physicists had ever heard of what is called the World Wide Web....
Now even my cat has its own page."* – BILL CLINTON

Social Media

It is no secret that social media changes constantly. In 2000, it virtually did not exist. In 2004, MySpace was king; by 2008, Facebook reigned supreme; in 2012, "hot codes," YouTube, and mobile media apps were tops. The key to effective social media and all communications is a clear, concise, and appropriate message that is regularly refreshed and distributed.

Website

In today's social media and online crazed culture, the Internet is a vital part of your campaign. Your website needs to have strong visual appeal. It will be far more than just an information tool. It will be your online fundraiser. Done correctly, it will bring volunteers to your camp as well as votes from people you may not have had the chance to meet. Don't cut corners or pinch pennies on your website. Do it right, from the start, and it will pay off manifold.

Get Multimedia Minded

Your website should feature a strong bio that is short and includes only relevant information, great pictures, and messages. Videos are inexpensive and easy to upload to a website. At a minimum, your site should have links to sign up volunteers, receive emails, and of course, a contribution link. Make an "Issues" page part of your website and share your position on each issue. People do not have time to search your entire site. Have headers that point out your issues to draw the reader's attention. Consider having a comment section so folks can email in their concerns; the intensity and frequency of comments can help guide your priorities and messages.

Email Blasts

Email blasts (our personal favorite) are one of the most effective communication tools available, and can put your message in front of many people in a flash. Information needs to be short and to the point. Never get into a cyber-war with any form of email. It will suck the life out of you and you will not gain a single vote. Keep the muzzles on your war dogs.

Facebook

There are a few key points to using Facebook. Users must register before using the site, after which they may create a personal profile, add other users as friends, and exchange messages. Additionally, users may join common-interest user groups, organized by workplace, school, or college, or other characteristics, and categorize their friends into lists such as "People from Work" or "Close Friends."

Twitter

Twitter is another great tool to send messages and gain followers. This online social networking service enables users to send and read super-short text-based posts of up to 140 characters, known as "tweets." Twitter provides you the ability to communicate with people who normally would not have the time to reach out to you. Notice what happens when you have reached the maximum number of characters.

> This is what 140 characters looks like. When you don't have much to say, 140 characters can seem like plenty. But if you run on, you get cut off.

YouTube

YouTube, a video-sharing website, is a great platform for reaching thousands of voters through video. Register to upload your videos to share your message and propel your campaign. Use tag lines to help people search for your videos. Make it simple, to the point, and attractive.

Smart Phone Applications

There is an app for just about everything, including this book. With the prevalent use of mobile devices and smart phones comes another social media tool called applications or apps. Check with a web designer to see if he or she can create an application for a smart phone for you. This is a great way to send messages, allow others to follow your campaign, and to contact you. Anytime there is a published update, it automatically updates the app, notifying your followers of any new information.

Post Responsibly

There are only two things that can never be taken back: bullets and words. Make sure when you use social media that you stay away from negative remarks. Pay attention to your opponent's social media, but never engage with them through any form of social media.

ANNOUNCE YOUR CANDIDACY

Carving a Path to Victory: Strategy is the Art of making use of Time and Space." – SUN TZU

YOU ARE ABOUT TO PUBLICLY REVEAL your decision to run for office. Now is not the time to be timid or modest about *winning* this race. If you've done the work outlined in the previous steps, then you're well prepared for the contest ahead. Take confidence in our simple step-by-step strategies—they have worked well for others and will work just as well for you.

BEFORE THE BIG ANNOUNCEMENT

Before you announce, make sure these two big items are checked off your to-do list:

1. File the necessary paperwork to receive contributions and collect as much money as you can. If you have not yet received permission to collect contributions, don't wait; obtain pledges that you can collect on later. If you plan to borrow campaign money, do it all up front.
2. The first minute that you can file for office, submit your paperwork.

File first, come out with a high-impact press release, and show you are well funded. This might cause some of the other candidates to pull out.

ROMANCE THE PRESS

Your marketing manager should be knowledgeable about press releases. This written communication is always directed at the news media to announce something that is newsworthy—like your bid for public office.

Typically, press releases are mailed, emailed, or faxed to specific editors or reporters at newspapers, magazines, television and radio stations, and online media.

Quickly and enthusiastically get to the point in your press release. It should set the tone of your upcoming campaign by clearly stating the reasons you are seeking office. Emphasize your two or three message points and how your values line up with those of the voters.

Romance the heck out of it. For instance, in the survey we mentioned earlier, 63 percent of voters stated that civic and community involvement influenced their votes. So be sure to include all civic duties that you have performed.

Send lots of photographs with your press release. Photos help establish your image. Capture several memorable images—*Kodak* moments. The best photos include your family, and don't forget Fido, unless of course Fido is a pit bull. People think of stability and compassion when they see your spouse, children, and pets. Pictures of you speaking to students, meeting people, coaching children's sports, working in the community, riding a horse, sitting behind your desk, and attending church are just a few examples that can set a positive image.

GET THEM TO RECOGNIZE YOUR NAME

Both marketing and branding are critical elements to winning. Some people don't know, or don't care, about the political issues at all. For those people, name recognition means everything. We had our work cut out for us when it came to getting Matt quick name recognition in the community. His well-known opponent ran his campaign as if he were the mighty protector of the rural culture. The community thrived on its rural character and was protective of the horse ranches in the area. Local sports teams enjoyed a huge, loyal following.

Fortunately, Matt had the right background. He was already a strong advocate of the culture, grew up on a horse ranch, and was a football coach for more than 300 local kids for more than 10 years. We presented the new unknown candidate in his college football uniform. We had another shot of Matt in his early years riding a horse on the ranch where he grew up. Another recent picture of him and his wife in a barn with their two dogs was highly effective. We painted a picture of the real Matt and it got him instant name recognition. He was immediately a person to whom people could relate. He was one of them.

SHOW YOUR GUNS WITH EARLY ENDORSEMENTS

Making a strong presence early in the race means showing up on day one with endorsements. Announcement day will be a good time to do a little name-dropping by mentioning your well-known and respected endorsers in your announcements and early literature based on the campaign strategy you crafted with your A-Team. Show your opponent that you have the muscle and resources to take you to victory.

USE YOUR WEBSITE AND SOCIAL MEDIA

Your website should be complete and ready to launch before your big announcement. All of your messages to the public (website, Twitter, Facebook, email-blasts, press releases, blog, etc.) saying "Hello, my name is _Add Your Name_ and I'm in it to win it," should be prepared and approved by your appropriate staff well in advance

★ HOW TO MAKE YOUR ANNOUNCEMENT A BIG SPLASH

- Invite lots of media with pre-sent press releases.

- In the press release, name your campaign manager and get a few quotes from significant community influencers who are supporting you.

- Bring lots of people with you to the announcement location.

- Make a show of it and bring a photographer.

- Send a subliminal message to your potential opponents that you are well-funded and have an army of supporters ready to fight for you.

- Wear a big name tag and an even bigger smile.

- If allowable, cover the city or county with your signs the night before.

- After the announcement, send another press release with good photos of the event.

of your announcement date. Your media contacts will provide your marketing manager their required lead times for press releases and news spots.

On day one of your public race, send out your digital announcements early. And for goodness sakes, make sure that your online system for receiving and tracking donations works!

Provide ways for supporters to make donations such as online by credit card, debit card, and PayPal, or by mail using a check or money order (if permitted under local laws). Include brief instructions on how to sign up to volunteer or to request signs.

If there is ever a time for the "WOW" factor, this is it. Prepare for it well in advance and come out with guns blazing. Put the incumbent and other challengers on notice that you're "in it to win."

 The announcement sets the tone of your campaign. Make sure that all communication tools are in place before you announce. Issue a press release that incorporates pictures and messages that appeal to the voters, and make sure that your announcement has an impact throughout the area.

STEP 8
CONNECT WITH THE BOTTOM 80 PERCENT

"Politics is the gentle art of getting votes from the poor and campaign funds from the rich by promising to protect each from the other." – OSCAR AMERINGER

WE'VE SPENT A LOT OF TIME TALKING about voters in the bottom of the Pyramid—the Bottom 80, as we've called them. By not wasting precious time planning our campaign around friends, family, and current supporters, we've narrowed our scope to the 80 percent of voters who count.

Historically, people voted because it was an American obligation, if not a patriotic duty. They voted for the candidate who best fit the job. In the 21st century, many voters don't feel that same obligation. When they do vote, they are more focused on what's in it for them. They question, "Why should a person even bother to vote?" Many can't find a compelling reason, and therefore opt to stay at home on Election Day.

As a candidate you must now meet that challenge and ask yourself, "Why should a person bother to vote for me? And by the way, who and where are these people?" Thus begins the Pyramid Principle process. Identify the bulk of the voters, home in on their needs, and create a campaign strategy that touches their lives. This will define your Pyramid Principle campaign.

The 3 Keys
1. Perform the precinct analyses.
2. Prepare the voter history reports to identify voters to contact.
3. Contact the voters.

Now, we've said it before and we'll say it again. Campaigning is marketing and salesmanship. You need to know two important things: who the customers are and where they are located. The precinct analysis and voter history reports provide both answers. Simply stated, without putting them in place, you cannot make the Pyramid Principle work. The Pyramid has four sides: the base that holds the formula for winning the most votes, the left side that is the precinct analysis, the right side that provides the voter history report, and the back that holds your campaign strategies. Take away any of the four and the Pyramid collapses.

PRECINCT ANALYSIS

Prior to launching your campaign, do a precinct analysis to determine where the bulk of voters are located. The analysis should include the congressional district, city precinct (ward), neighborhood, and street. This analysis is going to be the district map. Simply hang it on the wall and apply the critical information on an overlay covering the map. You will quickly see the neighborhoods, right down to the street you want to target.

The district map can be found at your local elections office, county engineer's office, tax assessor's office, or the city community development department. The district map will identify the voter districts by number and show boundaries of each district and the cities assigned to it.

Next, obtain a map of the precincts of interest and overlay it onto the district map. Outline or color each voting precinct on the master map overlay. The size of each precinct will be revealed, making it possible to compare them from largest to smallest, based on residency.

The precinct map provides greater detail about where target voters live and vote. This ward map zooms in on the layout of streets, providing street names, polling locations, location IDs, and addresses.

Okay, so now that you know the whereabouts of your voters, let's get to know a bit about them and their voting patterns.

VOTER HISTORY

To get this analysis done, you *must* obtain a *voter history report* on your soon-to-be-fans. This step is critical.

For a fee, you can obtain the voter history report from your local election office, political party, or through a private company which can be found on the internet. The voter history report provides critical information that will reveal to you voting activity over past elections. Operating without the voter list would be like trying to drive your car without an engine.

A report can be generated to obtain whatever type of information you need about voters by specifying a combination of the following criteria:
- Voting district(s) or precinct(s).
- Voter demographic data (age, sex, race).
- Party affiliation.
- Registration date.
- Voting history for a specific election.

Reports may be sorted in one of the following orders:
- Alphabetically by name.
- Alphabetically by residence/street (this is your walking list).
- Alphabetically by precinct or party.
- Household (voters with the same residence address).

More than likely, you will be interested in a report that lists current registered voters, as well as those who have voted in a particular election, and/or those who have received absentee ballots. The objective is to find out who the real voters are in your district. Match this information with your precinct analysis and voila! Continue to run all the pertinent voter history lists to fill your master map.

WILL THE REAL VOTER PLEASE STAND UP?

Perhaps the most important first step is to analyze the voter file. You need to establish your "win number." The win number is how many votes you need to win your election. The voter file is your history book and GPS system. It will tell you how many people vote, who they are, and where they live. Think of it this way: when you decide to travel someplace new, the first thing you do is determine your route. The voter file is the same thing. In our game, the key is votes. Remember the Pyramid—go where the votes are and leave the rest alone.

You may be asking yourself, "How do I analyze the voter file?" The first step is determining how many people are likely to vote. Barring a major event, our experience tells us that at least 90 percent of the people who are going to vote in your election voted in other recent elections. Here are three tips on how to analyze the voter file:

Tip 1: Who is a likely voter?

We start by looking at people who voted in at least two of the last four similar elections. This will probably yield a count higher than the actual number who will turn out, but this is a good thing. Although you only need 50%+1 in most cases (you might simply need a plurality to win; the rules vary from community to community), you always want to work more voters than you need.

Tip 2: Consider the Drop-Off Rate

Most voter files are only going to tell you how many people voted on Election Day. You can also obtain the total count of people who voted in a specific election. This information is generally obtained from your local elections office. Once you have this count, you can calculate the drop-off rate for your race. The drop-off rate is the percentage of voters who skip your race when they vote. ***REMEMBER THE PYRAMID.*** You want to focus first on the areas with the highest turnout and lowest drop-off rate. ***GO WHERE THE VOTERS ARE.*** Areas that are low turnout and have a high drop-off rate should be near the bottom of your list of targets.

Tip 3: Understand the Voter Demographics

Once you know the who and the where of your likely voter pool, you need to understand the demographics. Does your voter population skew old or young? What are their political leanings? What is their racial composition? Are there more women than men? Understanding your voter demographics will help you create the master plan.

The lesson here is that the citizens who actually vote are your primary targets, as it is likely they will vote in your election. Those who have a trend of not voting should not be targeted for personal contacts. You can only knock on so many doors, so knock on voters' doors and pass up the others. This same group of real voters will also get more attention through your other forms of communication. If time and funds are available, you can go back and work on the others in hopes that you can influence them to vote and, of course, vote for you.

By using the voter history list and the precinct information, and applying them to the master map, you will start the planning phase of your campaign, prioritizing your activities. This simple process takes away the guessing game and gives you clear direction to target voters by precinct. It will provide information needed for voter communications, including phone banks, campaign mailers, phone calls, and social media. And, of course, it will be your guide for all those home contacts and where to place signs. In a nutshell, it will direct where you and your team will spend the majority of the campaign's time and dollars.

It may surprise you that only about 50 percent of the people vote, even in a presidential election. During non-presidential election years, the figure is around 37 percent. For primaries and special elections, cities are lucky to get 20 percent of their citizens to vote. Do the math. Do you really want to spend your resources on around 50 to 60 percent of the people who aren't going to vote?

Now that the target market of voters has been identified, it's time to reach them through whatever means necessary. If you want the simple formula for victory, grab your voter list, which is the most important tool in the box, and start knocking on doors.

THE KNOCK-AND-TALK METHOD

The knock-and-talk method is the heartbeat of the Pyramid Principle campaign. During your neighborhood canvassing, you will quickly realize the importance of the precinct analysis and voter lists. Don't be overwhelmed. Remember, you will not knock on every door in the neighborhood. Prepare a well-defined plan and use your volunteers. You should have a driver and a couple of helpers to assist you.

Your driver will control the target homes you visit and keep you on a productive path. You will make the knock and talks. Keep it short and to the point as you hand prospective voters your campaign push card. Always ask for their vote on Election Day. If they agree to put a sign in their yard, your volunteers will do that on the spot. If no one is home, leave a pre-signed door hanger. Your driver and helpers can leave door hangers at the homes that are not on the voter list as you all move throughout the neighborhoods.

Do we even have to mention a clean car and an immaculate appearance? Remember to wear your name tag! Make sure your volunteers have a campaign button, t-shirt, or a name tag that identifies them as members of your team.

DON'T REINVENT THE WHEEL

It's time to go back and repeat a couple of recommendations that work. As we said earlier, we have tried and tested these methods numerous times. We have gone through the hard knocks. We have lost some, but we have won more times than not. Maybe it's because we listened to the voters. But this we do know, and it is worth repeating: have two or three strong message points, and follow the Pyramid Principle and other strategies outlined in this book.

Outside of the Pyramid Principle, some tactics work well, while others are a waste of time and money. Is following the Pyramid Principle the only way to win? Not at all. But time

★ **TOP 3 REASONS WHY PEOPLE VOTE FOR ONE CANDIDATE OVER ANOTHER**

1. The candidate has strong message points that align with voter priorities.

2. Voters have met the candidate.

3. Voters have relied on an influencer/ endorser they trust.

and time again it seems to bring the most votes at a very low cost. It certainly works best in local elections.

Campaigns for different public offices, geographic areas, and local issues may require a modified strategy. For example, if you are running for a county or state office or are in a large city, you will likely not have the time to visit many of the voters at their homes. Nevertheless, the basic need for voter contact does not change. You just have to do it in other ways to cover the masses. The best way, and something that should be part of your daily routine, is to make phone calls. You have to plan and be disciplined. *MAKE 100 PHONE CALLS PER DAY, EVERY DAY. NO EXCEPTIONS.* This ranks as our #2 must-do right behind personal contacts. *These calls are essential, even when running in small, local elections. You will not be able to knock on every door, so use your voter contact list and make those phone calls.*

A BIRTHDAY SURPRISE

In one campaign we are aware of, it was virtually David vs. Goliath. In this case, David outsmarted and outworked his opponents. One of the most effective things he did was to send a birthday card to every single voter in his district and then follow up with a phone call. He spent a full year doing it so that he made contact with virtually every voter twice, once with the card and once with a live phone call. It was well received, and of course, it was personal, which touches both the heart and the memory.

I received a call from my neighbor one Sunday morning, and she asked, "Do you know this David guy?" I said, "Yes." I could hear the excitement in her voice as she went on to say. "Well, he just called me on my birthday, and I received a card from him earlier in the week. We had a nice conversation and he let me know he was running for office. He was sincere and I did not feel like it was even close to a solicitation call or anything like that." With a little more intensity she said that her own son didn't send her a card or bother to call her. She said that she was being given five minutes to talk about anything she wanted to, at her church, later that day. (The attendance in that church is over 300 people.) She said she was going to talk about the nicest man she has visited with in a long time and would ask church members to vote for him next month. (Can you say "snowball effect"?) Typically, those people will tell others. Did David just pick up 300 to 400 votes with one phone call? Although the race was close, David beat two Goliaths on Election Day.

SCHOOL BUS STOP CANVASSING

Another way to put the Pyramid Principle of personal contact in action is to visit with parents at school bus stops. To call it a major vote getter would be an understatement. Cover these stops like a blanket because you have a captive audience, mostly voters. Plan it so that when the bus makes its rounds you will be a few miles in front of it and will have about 15 minutes to meet with parents as they wait with their children for the bus. Over time, you will be able to visit all the area bus stops. The key here is to get someone you or people on your team may know in the neighborhood to join you and introduce you to the parents. Wear your name tag and be sure to hand out push cards. Have signs handy, and if parents agree, your on-site helpers should walk back to their homes and install them.

LETTER FROM A NEIGHBORHOOD LEADER

Voters respond best to personal contact with the candidate. But your support team can also serve as influencers and bring voters to your side. The following is an example of a letter that one neighborhood leader sent to every home in her neighborhood. It is interesting to note that this is the largest voting neighborhood in the city, and they turned out in mass on Election Day and overwhelmingly supported the two candidates mentioned in the letter. Both won.

> *The November 8 election for city council is more important than most people realize. Yet the turnout at the polls will probably be small.*
>
> *This is unfortunate because the stakes are high. This election will determine what our city will become; not only over the next four years, but also over the next two generations. That is because our City Council will decide whether Mayberry will be financially viable in the years ahead. I urge you to vote for John Smith and Mary Doe.*

John has a solid financial background, and Mary is a civil engineer specializing in municipal projects such as parks, transportation systems, and educational facilities. We need their talents and experience on our city council.

The stakes are particularly high for our neighborhood. We are the city's largest neighborhood, and our voice must be heard. We have been largely ignored by the incumbents that John and Mary will face on November 8.

The city's Comprehensive Plan says expenses will begin to exceed revenues in less than two years. This is a looming financial disaster. Our city residents already pay 85 percent of our property tax burden, which is far higher than surrounding cities. Unless we find additional sources of revenue, our individual taxes will surely increase even more just to maintain our existing services.

John and Mary have the experience, commitment and conservative values we need on our City Council. They will not let our city slip into financial chaos.

The incumbents they face are well-entrenched politicians. John and Mary are therefore at a disadvantage on Election Day. That is why it is so important that you and your neighbors vote.

Politicians need to be held accountable. The incumbents have had their opportunity to serve, and they did not do the job. We need a change.

The choice is clear. Please vote for John Smith and Mary Doe on November 8. Visit their websites for further details about their plans for our wonderful city. Smith4xxxxxxx.com and Doe 4xxxxxxx.com.

Your neighbor,
Sally Cole

 There is nothing that brings votes like a personal contact. Do your precinct analysis. Use the voter history reports to identify the voters you must contact. Then go make those personal contacts.

STEP 9
FIGHT CLEAN

"Instead of paying good money to have your family tree traced, go into politics. Your opponents will do it for you." – ANONYMOUS

MOST CAMPAIGNS START THE SAME, "We are going to run a clean campaign! No mudslinging. We will campaign on the issues." We preach the same thing and try our best to hold the line. We even contact the opponent and try to agree on ground rules: "We won't if you won't." And occasionally, it works out. If we know an opponent well and know they are going to play dirty, we offer them a special bargain: if they won't lie about us, we won't tell the truth about them.

On several occasions, incumbents have met with individuals planning to run against them and have talked them out of it. *It never hurts to ask, but never ever offer a quid pro quo to convince a potential candidate not to run.*

When the other side starts slinging mud, you must resist playing in their pigpen. In extreme cases, however, you may be forced to respond to opponents' attacks, especially if the attacks cause your polling numbers to drop.

 If you must respond to attacks, communicate only honest factual messages. Stay with the issues and your message—no low blows, and never attack the family.

WHEN THE MISSILES LAUNCH

Okay. Enough of the niceties and the naive thinking. Look up. The missiles are coming. Once attacks start, they can consume a campaign like the plague. Negative campaigning is a strategy in itself to get you off message and draw you into a fight. Your attacker plans for you to waste time and money countering their attacks. As a result, the process will suddenly dominate your campaign. Egos will get in the way of everything else and before you know it, your team will be hell bent to show the world who is right.

Great . . . Win the battle, win the war, but lose the election.

Supporters, who believed in your message, will abandon you when they see negative campaigning take over your platform. We have too often seen campaign teams meet to talk about productive action plans, but end up talking for hours about the evil opponent, thus stealing productivity away from the campaign. Swallow the pride, put your opponent on ignore, and go to work to get votes. Focus on the mission.

ANGER MANAGES EVERYTHING POORLY

Most campaigns are based on issues, but occasionally a negative statement about you will surface that starts the gossip flying and, even worse, draws media attention. It will make your blood boil, but be prepared to deal with it in a calm, professional manner. Don't let it get to you. Understand it is part of the ugly side of politics. Let your campaign manager deal with it. Regardless of the temptation to strike back, don't do it. Anger manages everything poorly. An experienced campaign manager is used to handling negative attacks and is well aware that there is plenty of time to respond. However, when a response is given, it should be on your terms, not your opponent's.

STAY COOL IN THE HEAT OF THE CAMPAIGN

When it is all said and done, campaigns are tough. You, your family, and your supporters are emotionally invested. There is risk in choosing to campaign for public office. If you win, your reputation is elevated because all those who supported you saw the fruits of their efforts. Their names are in the winning column together with yours. They believe you will make a positive difference in their community, and they are excited for the change.

On the other hand, if you lose, everyone is disappointed. Your shared vision for the community will not happen, and everyone knows it. Time will go by before you can run again. All the time you spent campaigning will have been a great experience, but anything more that comes of it will come from the hands of others. What's more, if you have some campaign debt, you will have a difficult time raising additional funds to pay it off.

Your opponent faces the same risk. As the campaign takes on a life of its own, there will come a time when you will to have to look deep inside yourself and decide who you are, what you believe, and if the ends justify the means. We firmly believe that competition doesn't build character, it reveals it. As much as people don't believe it can be done, we know that you can win AND still look yourself in the mirror when the election is over.

So, what will be your stance? You vow to run a clean campaign now, but what happens if the other side gives in to win at all costs? The risk is real. You may agree with us that the risk is real while you are reading this book, but you won't know how real that risk is until you FEEL it in the heat of the campaign.

What are some of the tactics that will be used against you? They take many forms, and some can be quite imaginative. In every case, each tactic is either an attempt to give your opponent more exposure or define you as someone who will be damaging to the community. Here are just a few that may pop up and give you and your campaign team pause:

- Creative photos.
- Misleading graphs.
- Subjective comparison charts.
- Imaginative automated-calls.
- Intimidation tactics during a debate.
- Breaking of campaign sign rules.

- Manufacturing false endorsements (such as police, fire, and public officials).
- Manipulation of the local media.
- Politicizing non-political events.
- Stealing your signs.

Your A-Team and volunteers want to see you win. They are emotionally and financially invested. That's a good thing. Before you decide your next steps, know that staying above the fray will bring you a ton of support and votes. How do we know? The voters told us. It's about winning the election, not a mud-slinging contest. One statistic that stood out in the survey was that over 70 percent of voters are turned off by negative campaigning.

THE JUST-DON'T-ANSWER TECHNIQUE

Don't answer negative attacks. Answering a negative attack or rumor will cause more harm than good. While the attack may feel harsh, most people will not see it or pay any attention to it. If you answer it, you've just added fuel to the fire and pretty much exposed negative information to others. It now has drama and interest and spreads like wildfire. In one example, an opponent was falsely accused of wanting to raise taxes. Acting out of anger and impulse, he put out a robo-call to 40,000 people saying someone was falsely telling everyone he would raise taxes and the fact is he would not. You guessed it— what most people heard was negative and tied his name to it. Even worse, they heard his name and something about raising taxes. Guilt by association?

 Never reinforce a negative message. Eat it and forget it. Your wasted effort is just part of another well-thought-out trap by the opponent!

GAINING A POSITIVE FROM A NEGATIVE

Negative campaigning on your part can actually help the opponent's branding. The reverse is also true. If people are talking about someone, that person's name is being acknowledged. Remember, only two letters separate infamous from famous.

Opponents who use negative attacks virtually beat themselves. By refusing to respond, you can take the high road and propel your campaign forward. We've seen it happen—the uglier the attacks, the lower the attacker sinks in the polls. Too often they get stuck in attack mode and won't change course even though the tactic is clearly backfiring. All you have to do is stay out of the mud and keep a muzzle on your own attack dogs.

CHARACTER WINS

People can tell when a person is genuine. Be yourself, and don't ever be a politician. There is a difference between a public servant and a politician. Honesty builds trust and faith and that reflects strong character.

FOCUS ON YOUR MESSAGE

The media will bring a lot of attention to your campaign. Get to know all your local media people. Work with them, be available, take their calls, give them straight honest answers, and always have an updated press release to hand to them. Make them your best friends. They can make or break you. If you dodge them or lie to them, they will bury you in a heartbeat. Never cause a reporter to miss a deadline. However, as we mentioned earlier, don't let them or anyone else asking questions of you get you off message. Understand the art of bridging: transitioning from an unrelated or negative question or statement back to your intended message. This is where your programmed messages will come in handy. In the political jungle there are animals waiting to swallow you whole. The best way to defend against these predators is to bridge their attacks back to your message points. For example, your message is about the color blue. A reporter may state that some feel the color orange is better than blue. In your response you should acknowledge their point, then bridge back to your message of why blue is better. You know that controversy and drama sells. Interviewers want an exciting story and they are trained to lead you into something controversial.

Don't let them. They will know quickly if you are media savvy. Passion is good. Anger is not.

Dismiss and Leverage

When asked about something negative, the key is to dismiss the negativity and leverage the opportunity to say something positive that will benefit your campaign. For example, a question to the candidate might be, "I understand you were sued by your former business partner?" You would answer, "Yes. I won the case and believe frivolous lawsuits hurt small businesses and families, which is why I support tort reform."

TRAPPING THE RUTHLESS OPPONENT

Gathering intelligence plays an important role in trapping your opponent. Know the enemy as well as you know yourself. Your team should know everything about the opposition. Understand their history and monitor every move they make. It is easy to get a reading on your opponent from comments he or she makes to the media and the public, in mailers, email blasts, and websites. Are you listening? Make darn sure you don't put out damaging information through the media, mailers, emails, and websites that will burn *you* later. Don't get caught in their trap. It is in areas like this where candidates who aren't under the wing of a campaign manager normally go down in flames.

There are several ways to combat attacks and still keep your marketing

★ SIX MUST-DO'S TO SQUASH INVERVIEW ATTACKS

1. Be friendly and composed when challenged or asked a question.
2. Never show anger.
3. Pause and think about your response before you answer.
4. Restate the question or point as part of your response.
5. Bridge back to your message.
6. Leverage negative questions with positive statements.

positive. First, always counter with fact and truth. Remember Joe Friday on Dragnet? "Just the facts, and only the facts, Ma'am." This same thinking must apply if you have to go to counter measures. Make sure the right people on your team, especially your campaign manager and attorney, put their stamps of approval on anything that goes out.

Never Interrupt Your Opponent When He is Making a Mistake

The best traps are those that allow the opponent to walk right into them. The information used in traps normally comes from the opponent stating their platform and their campaign path. Understanding the opponent's path will allow you the opportunity to find where and what type of trap is needed.

We found that 91 percent of voters are influenced by a candidate's voting history, which could be detrimental for an incumbent. One opponent had a history of delay tactics and was anything but business- or growth-friendly. People remembered, and we made darn sure they did. We campaigned on a pro-business platform knowing we could direct our opponent's campaign strategy. Our opponent took it hook, line, and sinker. He continued to beat the drums on how the culture of the small town would be ruined if businesses were allowed. At that point, he was in the trap and had nowhere to go. His platform was established and we virtually defined his campaign. His old tactics to play on the fear of the voters no longer played well. He beat himself.

USE YOUR CAMPAIGN MANAGER FOR DAMAGE CONTROL

Most candidates will make mistakes along the way. The media may twist your words, or the other camp may put out false information. Be prepared to do damage control. Too quick of a reaction will normally dig a deeper hole, leading you to play right into the opponent's hand. Many hours will be spent in the tit-for-tat scenarios that will follow and, of course, you will become the town clown. The media will have a field day. This is where professional campaign managers come in. You and your campaign manager will assess the risk to determine if damage control is needed; in many cases it may not be. For instance, negative information may hit only 100 people, but sending out a rebuttal may cause it to hit 500 additional people—now 600 people are aware. What would have been a low- or no-risk incident has now been elevated into something substantial. The campaign manager will also steer you out of and away from traps and help you clean up any self-made messes.

One thing we hope for is that the opposition will go low and get sucked into running a dirty campaign. You never know. We might even throw out a few teasers just to stir things up a bit. Don't allow the competition to blast you the day before an election, which is a strategy in itself. You want to hold those cards, not them.

STEP 10
RIDE THE ROAD
TO VICTORY

"Success is getting what you want;
happiness is wanting what you get." – DALE CARNEGIE

THE BIG DAY HAS ARRIVED. Although early voting is on the increase, nationwide statistics show that 70 percent of the voters still vote on Election Day. Don't even think of relaxing a little. Election Day demands that you and your supporters work the hardest and put in the longest day of the entire campaign. You will need to cover those polls like a blanket, from the early hours before they open until the bell rings and they close the doors. The long-awaited finish line is in sight and it's time to sprint. Don't let up at the eleventh hour because this is the grand finale and your last chance to garner votes. The experts claim that if you don't do anything else right, you need to have your act together on this day to give yourself the best chance of winning.

GET OUT THE VOTE (GOTV)

Getting your supporters to vote is the obvious top item on the agenda. Send them an email blast the night before and several times during the day of the election, thanking them for their support and reminding them to vote. Ask them to call all of their contacts with the same message. "Please vote today and vote for our candidate." Look at the statistics—it's amazing how many people don't vote, which is exactly why the best candidate doesn't always win. Voters need prodding, and at this point there is nothing to lose. The election is a contest of who gets their voters out, plain and simple. Call, email, use social media, put up a blimp, drive through neighborhoods with a bullhorn. Do whatever it takes to get YOUR voters out!

DISTRICT CAPTAINS RULE!

Planning for Election Day can be a daunting task, not to mention the major challenge of assigning district captains to every voting precinct. For that reason alone, planning for Election Day has to start many weeks ahead. You may ask, "What do district captains do?"

Having recruited and prepared their army of volunteers throughout the campaign, district captains move into high gear as Election Day nears. They work with the sign manager and his army to coordinate the placing of campaign signs and sign wavers at each precinct. On the big day, they oversee all precinct activities, from assigning volunteers to ensuring compliance to the rules at voting locations. After the polls close they gather the results and report them to the campaign manager (and to no one else). Finally, the district captains work with their volunteers to collect and store all the campaign signs. Whew! Each polling place needs a captain and each captain needs a team—make that an army. Remember all of those people who asked how they could help? Sign them up from day one. Keep them involved throughout the campaign and make sure they show up on Election Day. They are free to recruit their own volunteer armies on Election Day—more is better.

District captains should contact volunteers often throughout the campaign to ensure they are still on board to volunteer. Do not allow your captains to wait until the last week or you may wind up being out there by yourself. Speaking of being out there, you and your family need to be on the front line from opening to closing. *Voters (and your volunteers) want to see you;* therefore, time your visits. Make the rounds, but be aware of prime time. Be at school precincts early in the morning and mid-afternoon when parents vote as they drop off their children and pick them up at school. Then spend the majority of your time at the largest precincts. Make sure you thank all your volunteers on the line and encourage them to call their friends and neighbors throughout the day to get them to the polls to vote.

SIGN DUTY AT THE POLLS

Encourage volunteers to wear the candidate's shirts and hats on Election Day. The first shift of volunteers should arrive at the poll several hours before the polls open and, along with the sign teams, place signs in the ground at all entrances to the polling place. The largest signs should be placed closest to the voting area; keep in mind it is illegal to have campaign material closer than 150 feet (this may differ by state) from the edge of the building where voting takes place. This is referred to as the forbidden "red diamond" area.

Sign-Waving Posts

Station three to four sign volunteers closest to the polling location, with others lining the roads leading to the precincts. Post your big signs in the ground at the first and last positions. Volunteers should stand near the traffic lane and hold signs, smile, and wave their hands in a friendly way. Do not wave the signs at motorists. It upsets them.

Ask every man, woman, and child on the campaign team to make as many personalized homemade signs as possible that they can use at the voting locations on election day. Show the voters: "VFW supports Matt," "Firefighters voting for Matt," "Vets for Matt," "School teachers for Matt," "Farmers

★ SIGN WAVING DON'TS

1. Do not wave the sign in front of cars.
2. Do not yell at cars or people going to vote. Be respectful. Yelling while waving signs is intimidating and may backfire, costing you votes.

for Matt," "XYZ neighbors for Matt," "Retirees for Matt," etc. More is better. Elderly folks, people in uniforms, other elected officials, and influencers in the community make great sign holders. Ask them to be there during prime times—the first two hours after the polls open, lunch hour, and the last two hours before the polls close. Several of our volunteers brought their big furry dogs. They became a focal point. One of them put a candidate t-shirt on her dog.

Having each voting location staffed with volunteers is the best way to go. However, if enough volunteers aren't available, select the voting precincts that showed the highest number of voters in the previous election and assign volunteers to work those locations.

COUNTING THE VOTE

At the end of the day, when all the voting precincts have closed, it is time to collect all the signs and get the results. The volunteers are tired and ready to see if all their hard work has paid off. Many voting jurisdictions will have all votes accounted for and the results within an hour after the polls close. The district captain, or other designated person, will stay behind to get the results that will be posted at the voting precincts and will relay them to the campaign manager. This process is the fastest way to get the results. Waiting for radio, TV, or internet updates can take hours.

The victory belongs to those who persevere!

OFF TO THE VICTORY PARTY

The victory party should be a location that is well known and can hold a large number of people. Every campaign supporter, contributor, and volunteer should be invited to attend. The location should have TVs so people can watch the election results roll in.

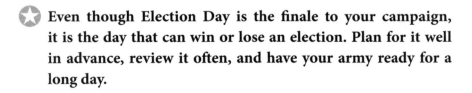 **Even though Election Day is the finale to your campaign, it is the day that can win or lose an election. Plan for it well in advance, review it often, and have your army ready for a long day.**

It's ok to enjoy your success, but you should never quite believe it.

IT'S NOT OVER YET

Just when you thought it was over, your campaign has to go into overdrive. Retiring your debt should be near the top of your "things to do list." Campaign debt is important, but the debt of gratitude to everyone who helped you along the way is far more important. Your family, friends, A-Team, and all your volunteers need a special "Thanks," if not a hug. The voters you contacted during the campaign also need personal thanks: a phone call, an email, or even a thank you card. Let them know that you will repay their support by working hard on their behalf. If you can afford it, maybe even place a small, personalized, notice in the paper thanking all of your supporters. Believe it or not, your next campaign just started, so lock in those votes you worked so hard to get. Your supporters will remember that "thank you" (or lack thereof).

 Don't make the fatal mistake that so many do by thinking you pulled off that victory by yourself. Many people worked very hard to get those votes. Treat all those who helped you along the way very well, or you may be a one-time winner and very lonesome in your next campaign.

POST-CAMPAIGN ANALYSIS

So, when the polls close and the votes are counted, every campaign team sits around the war room with the same questions. The winners want to know what caused the victory and the losers want to know what caused the loss. Explaining a loss is usually easy, with the obvious question being, "Did we beat ourselves?" However, the post-campaign analysis takes you through a detailed review of the campaign. We advise candidates, campaign managers, and A-Team members to keep good notes throughout the campaign. Notate all the things that went well or what contributed to a positive outcome. On the other hand, notate what things did not go so well or contributed to a less than an ideal outcome. These notes are not for pointing the finger, but should be used to develop a constructive debriefing that will prove to be a valuable tool in preparation for future campaigns.

Each race will be a little different, but the following is a pretty good example of a debriefing document we chose at random from the high stack of notes we have collected over the years.

WHAT WENT RIGHT?

1. Strong press releases and social media due to an experienced scriptwriter on the team.
2. Strong campaign manager.
3. Professional mail pieces sent in a timely manner and highly effective postcards.
4. Stayed positive; did not get sucked in the gutter; stuck to the issues.
5. Stayed proactive, not reactive.
6. A great sign placement team headed up by dedicated captains.
7. Good worker bees (I give the credit to them for our win).
8. Was able to get the mayor and strong endorsers to come out for us; a few had fundraisers.
9. Because we built strong media relationships, the newspapers favored us (this was huge).

WHAT WENT WRONG?

1. Got a late start.
2. Delayed bringing in a campaign manager (major error).
3. Blindsided by opposition's strong social media blitzes.
4. Went way over budget due to late start and had to play catch up.

WHAT I WISH WE HAD DONE

1. Used our volunteers more efficiently.
2. Secured voters list earlier so we could have segregated it into different blocks (i.e., senior voters).
3. Nailed down sign locations sooner, should have called my previous sign location people.
4. Wasted less time reading blogs.

5. Avoided reinventing the wheel. Should have stuck to the basics (I overspent especially in a panic the last week). Will I ever learn to plan?

HOW DO I GET READY FOR THE NEXT ELECTION?

1. Build stronger relationships with the factions that supported my opponent.
2. Increase my email list; get updates from the city/county/state.
3. Send out newsletters updating citizens on accomplishments and encourage input from them.
4. Hold at least two town hall type meetings in my district.
5. Send out emails with breaking news and upcoming city events.
6. Become more involved with local charities.
7. Build better relationships with local media.
8. Become involved in local schools and their activities.
9. Review my campaign statements and be sure that I follow through when in office.

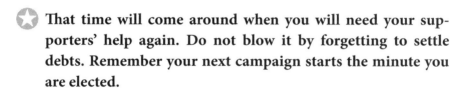 **That time will come around when you will need your supporters' help again. Do not blow it by forgetting to settle debts. Remember your next campaign starts the minute you are elected.**

Build a Platform for the Next Phase

When you arrive at your newly won office, keep one thing in mind: how long you stay will be based on your results and how well you communicate. Communication while in office is the key to building a foundation of supporters. It is also the cheapest and easiest "best kept secret" because it is not common for elected officials to worry about communication until it is close to re-election time. Use social media and newsletters year-round to keep citizens updated on government affairs and other matters of interest. As you build a following and the next election rolls around, campaigning will be much easier. You've heard the comment, "It must be election time again because that person is out and about talking with groups and getting stuff done." If you communicate year-round, then that type of statement or stigma won't apply to you. Your communication and outreach will give you a commanding jump on anyone with an eye on your office and also bring you a level of support that will be needed at election time.

GIVE YOURSELF AN ADVISORY COMMITTEE

People who support a campaign, a cause, or some other movement want to see that cause end with a good result and say they were involved. Those who aspire to be great leaders in the community need to have the ability to listen. As a newly elected official, surround yourself with a few strong people to help you make important decisions as you work your way through your new role as a public official. Tap into the people who supported you by creating an advisory team. Meet on a regular basis—maybe once each quarter to talk about important matters. The advisory committee should consist of people you trust and who support you. You'll want to make them your stakeholders as you successfully serve your term, or terms, in public office.

Congratulations on a job well earned!

 Re-election is just around the corner, so remember what comes around goes around. Build a foundation to keep supporters involved through town hall meetings, newsletters, and social media.

We know a single book cannot cover all the things a campaign requires. We also know that different applications work in different areas for different offices. We hope this book was a help to you. Now, with all the integrity in the world, go do the right thing and bring honor to yourself and the office you just won.

Be Awesome!